LISA H

M000211953

## ABIDING STRATEGIES

# BUILD YOUR BEST
# BUSINESS FOUNDATION

SAPPHIRE ENTERPRISES, LLC

ABIDING STRATEGIES — BUILD YOUR BEST BUSINESS FOUNDATION
©2021 Lisa H. Harrington & Abiding Strategy
AbidingStrategy.com

Published by Sapphire Enterprises, LLC (d/b/a Abiding Strategy)

Library of Congress ISBN  978-1-7343836-2-1
  1. Business   2. Leadership   3. Mentoring & Coaching

Book design by Diane Boskovich & DMP Publishing
DMPpublishing.com

Imagery purchased through AgeFotostock.com
(Cover: *Pantheon in Rome by Romas* and *Binary Code Computer by Ihorsvetiukha*)


*Printed in the United States of America*

*For My Husband*

I am a Board member of *Grapevine Relief and Community Exchange (GRACE)*. GRACE serves all in need, primarily in Grapevine, Texas and the surrounding cities. The services provided are very diverse and, accordingly, require a strategic plan that supports all the business units focused on those clients in need. The services provided include financial assistance, healthcare services, transitional housing, food, clothing, Christmas preparation for families, children lunches during summer months, and other critical necessities of those served.

I am personally proud of what GRACE does for our clients and am honored to be a member of this prestigious board. With that background, I was particularly interested in updating our strategic plan. Knowing the importance of this update, our board recognized the need for having an experienced facilitator to lead this critical process. After much discussion, it was unanimously agreed to hire Lisa Harrington to lead us through the process.

With that decision made, we rented a facility to hold this meeting and all board members attended with Lisa leading the effort. Our common goal was not only to update the previous plan, but to improve on that plan. Lisa was outstanding. She kept the group both on track and involved during the entire process. Lisa's suggestions during the process were all accepted by the group and when we finished the group discussion, we had a completely updated road-map beginning with an outstanding overall mission statement and continuing through the various diverse "pillars" needed to encompass our many operating units. We all felt wonderful with the final product and were excited to firm up the detail.

From my personal standpoint, having been in management for over 40 years, and completing many "strategic plans," I can categorically say that this process was, by far, the best I have been involved in. I have never come away from a strategic plan development process as excited as I was with this and that can be attributed to both the quality of our board and to Lisa's leadership. The entire experience made me very proud of the finished product.

— John Slocum, *GRACE Board Member*

[*] AUTHOR'S NOTE: This book was written so that any business can benefit from having a strategy. A FREE companion workbook is available for download at my website so that you can create your own plan!

ABIDING STRATEGIES: Build Your Best Business Foundation
*FREE Companion Workbook*

AVAILABLE for DOWNLOAD at:
AbidingStrategy.com

# INTRODUCTION

## Why ABIDING?

*ABIDING* comes from *my life verse* in the Bible:

**John 8:31-32**. [31] So Jesus said to the Jews who had believed him, "If you abide in my word, you are truly my disciples, [32] and you will know the truth, and the truth will set you free."

## Dictionary.com says the word *abide* means:

*verb (used <u>without</u> object),* **a·bode** or **a·bid·ed**, **a·bid·ing**.
to remain; continue; stay: *Abide with me.*
to have one's abode; dwell; reside: *to abide in a small Scottish village.*

*verb (used <u>with</u> object),* **a·bod**e or **a·bid·ed**, **a·bid·ing**.
to put up with; tolerate; stand: *I can't abide dishonesty!*
to endure, sustain, or withstand without yielding or submitting: *to abide a vigorous onslaught.*
to wait for; await: *to abide the coming of the Lord.*

*Verb Phrases*
**abide by,**

> 1. to act in accord with.
>
> 2. to submit to; agree to: *to abide by the court's decision*
>
> 3. to remain steadfast or faithful to; keep: *If you make a promise, abide by it.*

This is important to me, because when I help plan a strategy for a business, I want it to last, endure, and withstand all pressures. And in order for a strategy to work, *the team has to agree and remain steadfast to the purpose, values, and vision of the business* — the business needs to build an **ABIDING** foundation.

Whatever else makes up a business, we first start with the *human condition.* We acknowledge that the human element is unavoidable and precious. The way we do our work relies on our humanness. *There is no way to separate the human element, so it becomes a part of our foundation of becoming a great leader and running a great business.*

The people, the humans and all their quirks and awesomeness and foibles are the FOUNDATIONS of a business. All of the systems and products and sales tactics and marketing strategies and investments and money and loans and banking and board meetings and advertising and policies and procedures are all useless without understanding, first, the basic foundations of running a great business; which is to say, to understand the employees and customers and vendors and regulators and stakeholders. You have to know about the people first.

**So, I start with FOUNDATIONS because it builds the best business.**

The **FOUNDATION** of a business can get overlooked so easily. There is something about coming through a crisis that makes us reassess and review our situations. We want the opportunity to start fresh and try something new. Mentally, emotionally and even financially we get a clean slate. Budgets are zeroed out, goals are rewritten and scales are reset. Hope abounds.

It is great to spend some time exploring the newest and latest. It's fun and energizing. If we don't do that on a regular basis, we get stale and bored and productivity suffers. Human beings are meant to renew and adapt. Change is good!

But this comes with a warning: in the hustle of trying to find the "next best solution" to work its magic and solve all the problems left over from the year before, we often get further away from the basics: *a foundation that is firm, deep, solid, well-planned and meticulously built.* Remember, the process cannot be rushed and it's difficult because it takes time to build — great discipline is needed to stay the course.

**What are the *three critical elements* to build a strategy that will ABIDE?**

**Abiding Leadership** builds the strategy from the foundation up! The deeper, more difficult work of vision and values for creating a strategy comes first. This means that the work endures change and crisis, gets done effectively while the results are achieved and stakeholders are inspired.

An **Abiding Culture** brings together the communication that is vital to long term thinking. It communicates the intentions, brings all the pieces together for the process and helps hold accountability in check.

An **Abiding Crew** will be able to implement and execute the steps that are needed with passion and resolve, so that your firm can leave a real legacy for the world.

[Note: You'll notice that a few concepts seem to be repeated throughout the book. This just means we are considering all from a different perspective, stakeholder, or process. It also means that the concept is important!]

**So, in having to build that solid FOUNDATION: Where do you start and what are the steps?** What "materials" do you need? Because foundations must start at the beginning to be effective *(as author Stephen Covey would say: "Begin with the end in mind"),* that's where I'm going to start and it's the purpose of this book. ***Are you ready to begin?***

DEDICATION

FOREWORD
*by John Slocum*

# INTRODUCTION
*Why ABIDING?*

SECTION ONE* — PAGE 13
## YOU, THE LEADER
*Why LEADERSHIP is Like a HOUSE*

SECTION TWO* — PAGE 67
## THE BUSINESS
*Your BLUEPRINT for STRATEGY PLANNING*

SECTION THREE* — PAGE 99
## THE CREW
*Your BEST TEAM to Deliver THE VISION*

---

BONUS CONTENT — PAGE 119
MAGGIE: *Love As Leadership*
[IN THE STYLE OF MY FIRST BOOK]
*Taking in Strays: Leadership Lessons From Unexpected Places*

---

## ABOUT THE AUTHOR — PAGE 126

*FREE COMPANION WORKBOOK AVAILABLE
as downloadable/printable resource at:*
**AbidingStrategy.com**

## *The STRATEGY Includes*

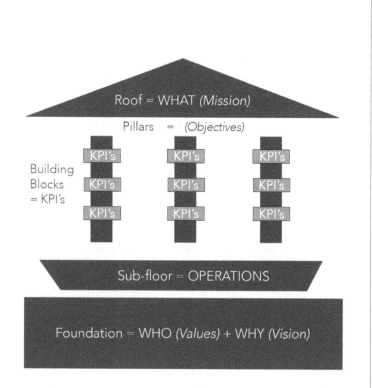

Everthing must rise from the FOUNDATION *(Values & Vision)*
and fit under the ROOF *(Mission)*.

# YOU, THE LEADER

## *Why LEADERSHIP is like a HOUSE*

I have worked a lot with Vision Mapping and other strategic, corporate structure type projects. It seems that everyone is trying to figure out how to re-build their organizations in what seems to be our new-normal environment, economically and otherwise.

What's worthy of sharing is the fact that the most effective way to start a new business, or hit re-set on an established business, is basically the same now that it has always been. I can share the process by comparing this to *building your house. So, I start with FOUNDATIONS because it builds the best business.*

**No matter what situation the economy is in, and in every state of progress in your business, _your house needs to stand on a very solid foundation_.**

*The very first step is to BUILD OUT YOUR FOUNDATION.* You can't raise the building until the foundation is built. A major remodeling job starts with checking to be sure the foundation is strong. For example, what would happen, if we built an addition to the side of the house but didn't expand the foundation, or dig a new one? The building addition would crumble.

*The foundation analogy* is our theme for a few reasons. Foundations are universal; every building must have one, no matter what its final purpose will be. No building can stand without them, and they take a long time to put down. Foundations are not the pretty part of the building, and they don't "sell." In some cases, the foundation will take as long to build as all the rest of the structure, even though it is rarely seen after completing. Foundations are easily forgotten — until they crack. And while every foundation is different in its application to the size and shape of the building, the basic physics are the same. No business can function long without strong foundations, and when you are analyzing the success or failure of a firm, it isn't long before foundational strengths or weaknesses come to light.

For our purposes, two questions must be answered to **BUILD OUR BUSINESS FOUNDATION**, and the documents that hold it up:

> (1) WHO are we
>           and
> (2) WHY do we exist

[Gather your team or representatives from parts of your team, and carve out some time to answer some questions together. *Access the companion workbook if you would like guidance on the process.*]

**There are two parts to a solid foundation.**

**(1) We start by defining WHO we are as an organization and entity by defining our *Values* and that leads us to an amazing culture**. The *values statement* is used more internally than externally, as a guide to the big decisions. *Values are: "Who are we?" "What lines won't we cross?" "How do we want the world to see us?" What are we willing to do or say?"* If we are describing ourselves to others, what do we say about our organization? This is difficult, because we want to start by talking about what we do, and how we do it. Those are the obvious things to discuss because they are tangible, and therefore easier to describe. But stick to your plan, and answer "who" first.

*List your values as a group.* Debate about which ones are most important in your outward and inward descriptions of your organization, and find the common ground. Write them down where everyone can see them every day, and live up to the *values* you profess.

**(2) Then we answer the question WHY? Why are we doing this? What is our *Vision*?** *Vision answers "what legacy are we leaving for the future?"* These answers will inform your decision about a public statement of your organization's *vision* and the world around it — guiding the type of culture you want in your shop. It's also the code by which your employees are hired, trained, disciplined or fired. It can even help define the types of clients you want to serve. Don't settle for the old, weary answers like "providing peace of mind" or "to make money" and such. Really dig down and answer why you do what you do on a more world changing level first. If we do not define ourselves, others will. And we may not like how they choose to define us.

[Read the book *Start with Why* by Simon Sinek if you want a little more info on "why to ask why."]

**With the answer to these two questions, WHO and WHY, you've just dug out your FOUNDATION: the two sets of decisions, phrases, attitudes and directions upon which you'll build the rest of your house.**

Foundation = WHO *(Values)* + WHY *(Vision)*

## ■ ABOUT PAPERWORK

PART OF CREATING THAT FOUNDATION INVOLVES A LOT OF PAPERWORK including but not limited to corporate bylaws, organization charts, standard operational procedures, job descriptions and the like. These are the rebar, plywood and 2x4s holding the foundation up, keeping the dirt from falling back down in the hole and creating the sub-floor for the building. Without it, everything gets very loose again and unorganized, and all of a sudden the dirt cannot resist the temptation to slide back down! This is part of working on the business, instead of in it, and it's easy to let these things slide to sell product, marketing the firm, and so on.

Many employees will never see the corporate by-laws, or job descriptions beyond their own, or the legal paperwork creating the corporation.

This is why it's so important to write the *Values* and *Vision* as public statements, staking claim to your *who* and your *why* early, and often. You need to be sure your foundation is accessible and visible.

*It might help to consider that the real value isn't in the paperwork at all.* What we want are the conversations that go around those that make such a difference in building out the foundation. *Communication is everything.* Done well, the best laid plans will be smoothly and effectively implemented. When communication is poor, nothing else works, no matter how well prepared it is. By putting those conversations and agreements in writing, we have a source of reference to go back to when we find ourselves sliding back into the hole or getting off track. *(Your attorney and accountant will also help.)*

## ■ TIME COMMITMENT

Another very important reason to prepare the foundation is the *long-term investment* you're making. A foundation takes a very long time to build. The taller or larger the building is, the deeper that foundation has to be. It can take as long to finish the foundation as it does to build all of the rest of the building! A fair amount of patience is required, because the urge is so strong to get on with the rest of the house. We don't really get to do anything exciting with that foundation, and generally speaking once it's done you never see it again. It's not pretty, and it isn't even something you have to refer to again very often for most parts of the organization.

Most foundations don't need re-digging if they were solid to begin with, even if they sometimes need a little leveling out or shoring up. A really well-built foundation will stand the test of time for hundreds of years.

One year in May, from my room in Toronto, I saw something that I wanted to share by way of analogy.

I was in the True North teaching a sales class. The course is twelve days long, taught for three days once per quarter. I was there a few times training trainers to facilitate the course. For the first year and a half, my room had overlooked the same general vicinity in downtown Toronto.

Like many big cities, Toronto is in a relatively constant state of construction. Cranes fill the air (not the feathered kind) and jackhammers sing. Our hotel was near the site of a new condominium and hotel complex where construction had begun two years before.

In six trips over 18 months, all we saw was the digging, pouring and stabilizing of the foundation of this massive structure. In all that time, not a wall or door or window was done. No bricks, two by fours or metal beams are in place. Not a drop of paint had been seen. Almost two years, and we still had only the foundation.

Now, to clarify: this is a massive structure that is going to be 60 stories or more, and which will include underground shops and a connection to the famous Toronto PATH. On inquiry, I was told *the foundation hole was nine stories deep.*

***I liken the hole that is dug for a foundation as our Vision & Values mapping process.***

The trouble with foundation holes is that they fall in on you if not done properly. Without structure and planning, and some support on the sides, a hole that deep fills itself in, and the building can never be put up.

The *vision* process can feel like nothing but the hole. Some might feel the analogy is a negative, but it's appropriate. It's the hardest step: to start. And, it's the easiest to give up on.

The structure around the hole that we dig, that keeps the whole thing upright are the *values* and *vision*. This begins the process of actually creating something. *We can decide a few things now.*

Foundations, values and the vision map required to build them, are best when firm, deep, and solid, well planned, and carefully, meticulously executed.

**Make the investment in a solid foundation.**

**Then the rest of the house comes together...**

Roof = WHAT *(Mission)*

## Next is the Mission Statement — the WHAT.

I see *the Mission statement* as the roof of the house; everything you do must fit somehow into and under that mission statement. **This is your answer to the question of WHAT.**

WHAT will we do to create the vision we have built so far, within the parameters of our WHY and sticking to our definition of WHO we are — writing that statement so that it becomes the guideline for everything else.

This one is quite familiar to most of us. Many already have a document, plaque, or web page dedicated to the mission. It's an externally used statement, telling the world "this is what we do." Who will be your customers? What geographic markets will you serve? This statement is short, to the point, and will fit on the back of your business cards. In larger or more complex organizations, there can be a mission statement for each division.

We are better served not to rush the process of building the base for our businesses or our families or our lives. A very high percentage of our time, effort and money need to be spent on the underpinning of our mission. Our structure, our business, simply will not flourish if we are not properly preparing the fundamentals.

Sometimes we do expand our *vision, values,* or *mission.* But we have to go back to square one each time we want to do that, and be sure we have put a solid foundation there, and that the entire structure still works. *If we don't have a roof, the rest of the building is ruined.*

## Next are the Objectives — the HOW.

**Objectives can be seen as the pillars which hold up our mission.** These are the three or four big picture functions of the organization, which we look back upon when we are deciding about priorities. Yours might be to: provide education, hire only the best employees, and value quality over quantity. So when you have limited resources, or budget requests are being compared, a great system to govern our efforts is to look back at the mission, or its strategic pillars, and ask ourselves "How does this project or budget fit our mission? Does it meet our values? Will it fulfill our vision?"

Pillars = (Objectives)

Your pillars or structural supports under the roof, growing up out of the foundation, answer the WHAT statement. *These structural pillars will guide the shape of the rest of the house.*

You'll also have walls and windows and doors that are your objectives such as: HOW, WHEN or WHERE. These are the tactical areas you'll need to address to be sure *the Mission* is accomplished.

At every step, it will be helpful to check against the structural pillars and make sure everything is fitting up under the roof. As your team or committee works along on the tactical objectives, they can continually check this point. It's easy to get off track, and start building additions to the house. If they look up sometimes to be sure they are still firmly upon the foundation of the *Vision and Values*, and under the roof of the *Mission*, they will be better equipped to complete the tasks in such a way that the *Mission* is accomplished.

Why do we go to all this effort? Because it provides the points of the compass of our organizational map for our employees. Before having to come ask you about their next initiative, they can screen against these three items. Everyone saves time and effort because they know not to come with anything that isn't meeting those vision, values or mission statements unless they can show some extraordinary justification.

## Key Performance Indicators — Building Blocks

**Building out the KPIs for your long-range planning is next.** *These are the building blocks of the plan.* What are the three to five measurable steps for each objective pillar? Everything is considered from client base to employees needed to financial impact of each and every decision. This is not a step to take lightly. Without this step, you simply careen into the future without direction. Even if your business is booming, and your profits are off the charts, you may be a runaway train heading for the washed out bridge! Don't use the excuse that you don't have time to plan. You have as much time as anyone else. You may get rich. But could you have been richer? Or could you have had a higher quality of life? Dream big, and adjust as you go.

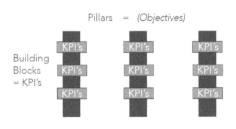

**Staffing is next.** Without them, nothing happens. Management is an art backed by science and we get better at it all the time. More on that later in the book.

> I was back in Toronto again that following November. That building which was only a foundation after the first 18 months was by then a towering 10 or more stories tall. All that in just six months. Once the foundation is complete, you can really make swift progress toward your success.

Plus, if you lay a strong foundation, building the right vision with the right values to bring on your people, great information, tools and foresight, you can be more confident in that plan succeeding in the long run, no matter how hard things are at the moment. How much do you really need to change in light of the economic climate, or the shift in your industry, or the world markets? Are you comfortable enough with your strategy plan to make simple adjustments, which you had in your contingency plans already, or is it really time to pull the thing out of the ground and start over? How can you be sure? Knowing when it's time to quit has value, but sticking it out for the long run can be much more rewarding.

*Beyond this, what are the steps? What materials do you need?*

You need great leaders.

You need a great culture.

You need a great crew.

*Let's start with your leadership…*

*Now that we've talked about the basic structure, how do we lead the way?* In our business planning the foundation is first, but it starts at the top, with the business leaders.

The point is that we, as leaders, have to be whatever our followers need us to be to accomplish the mission, secure the vision and live up to the values of the firm. At times, for example, we have to be flexible enough to let someone complete the project their own way. Other times, we have to be firm about methodology. It depends on the circumstances. Some would say that we have to be chameleons!* I tend to agree here. Even in a military setting, "my way or the highway" isn't really the best way to lead. Even on the battle-field adjustments must be made. Today, we may occasionally carry the military/hierarchy/organizational chart mentality a little too far, but it's got great merit for many situations.

This is where your flexibility has to come in, and the emotional balance, and the discipline to leave the plant in the ground and let it grow. As leaders, we act without panicking and make adjustments without bringing down the whole house. This means stopping to think, which is amazingly difficult in an era where we are supposed to tell our whole story in 140 characters or less. You really can't change the world with sound bites! Don't act without slow, prodding, thoughtful consideration from your own experience and that of those around you that you trust. Ask your peers & your staff. Read. Think.

Change for change sake probably won't help you. I have a lot of good friends in the IT world, and they'll all tell you that if a workflow isn't right before you automate, all you're

*[See *First, Break All the Rules* by Buckingham, et al]

going to do is speed up the mess you already have. Automation without careful planning won't help you, and slash and burn budgeting just to react to a bad economy won't either. You may need to stop the bleeding, but tourniquets can kill if not properly applied. So can corporate anorexia.

In today's "how fast can you change it up" environment it's difficult to resist the desire to keep pulling up the flowers to check the roots. But if you keep pulling that plant up you will kill it. If you don't build that very strong foundation to begin with, tapping into the amazing resources you have in yourself and your staff, you might not have confidence in the plan you have in place.

**Stop pulling up the flowers to check the roots!**
*Chris Almebein*

So, we are challenged right now as leaders, but we can help each other. Even if the foundation is actually rotten, we can probably fix it together, and if we do, we'll come out stronger and better on the other side.

*Remember the mission!* Allow plans to gel and grow and flourish.

# *LEADERSHIP Traits*

In the years I've been in the industry *(since 1983)* I've read hundreds of books and articles about leadership and what it means. We'll start with leadership traits; there's a long list of character traits necessary to be effective. Here's a random list of what leaders *must* be:

| | | |
|---|---|---|
| Effective | Talented | Strong |
| Efficient | Disciplined | Holistic |
| Patient | Persistent | Fearless |
| Flexible | Consistent | Decisive |
| Functional | Resourceful | Approachable |
| Emotionally Balanced | Fair | Focused |
| Empathetic | Ethical | Visionary |

We'll explore the traits together...and many more of course.

# Effectiveness

*Effectiveness is really the bottom line of leadership; if you aren't accomplishing the mission, something has to change.* It's pervasive, too. Effectiveness must be found in every layer of the projects, plans, and assignments. Just as you need proper plans to build the house, and a capable architect to create those plans, you need a builder with ability to read plans, make sure correct materials are ordered, manage proper installation, make sure work is done in the right order, and so on. It takes both to succeed: proper planning and proper implementation.

Much too often as leaders we focus on the plans themselves. Five-year plan? Check! Objectives laid in on a timeline? Check! Assignments to proper staff? Check! Accountability method? Um, huh? Gee...The same person who has the skill to lay out the strategic plan in your office may not be the right person to see it executed, or hold the crew accountable.

There is a natural tension between planner and builder, too. The person who laid out the plan may not have the best idea of what reality brings as those plans are implemented. And if there is a lack of flexibility on the part of the architect *(leader)* when the builder *(manager)* needs to make adjustments, it can lead to a lack of communication and a less effective end result. I've had a little experience with architect vs. engineer vs. construction manager. The builder often feels as though the practical side of construction isn't fully understood by the architect. And architects will sometimes say that construction managers are stuck in their old ways. This is a normal tension, and takes careful communication and patience to get the building off the ground.

Lots of leadership texts, including some of mine, talk about seeing things from "30,000 feet." But you can't actually see everything from up there. And it may have been a long while since you were down on the ground handling those day to day tasks. So, your vision of what is needed may vary from reality. Therefore, to truly get to effectiveness, you do need a myriad of talents. But we'll start with a quick reminder about the difference between leadership and management. It's critical.

There are a lot of great leaders who cannot manage, and vice versa. Unfortunately, too many people think that the two talents come from the same place. They do not. Managers are systematical, logical, process oriented and usually left brained folks. If that part of the brain does not dominate, you probably won't manage well even if you are a superior leader. The idea that the left/logical brain and the right/creative brain have different functions is quite real. It is well documented that we have a natural tendency to use one side more than the other.

But, unless someone has actually removed the left side of your brain, you still can use it! You just have to work a little harder to do so! A simple awareness of the need and a willingness to get help are usually enough. Exercises for your brain are available on the web, and just plain exercise in various forms challenges both sides of your brain. For example, if you are a runner, try something else, like Jazzercise, yoga or a dance class. Leaders who are heavily right brained can add systems and processes to their day to help them become more linear and logical, and therefore better managers.

When you can, in companies or departments that are large enough to justify this, you can have both leaders and managers as separate roles, as in...separate people! But in most cases, leaders must also manage, and managers need leadership skills. Now we have circled back, again, to the fact that to be effective, leaders need to have a variety of skills and talents.

## *Efficiency*

*Everyone knows that effectiveness and efficiency are separate aspirations.* We have all had experience with a situation when we were really quite efficient at doing exactly the wrong thing, and ended up with a fast, cheap, and completely inappropriate result.

So, too, the analogy between building a house and efficiency seems patently obvious. Energy efficiency has been a point of discussion in the US for decades, starting with the first time fuel prices went through the roof and some were warning that we were entering the "next ice age," right up to where everyone thought "global warming" was the crisis. Finally, we realized "climate change" might just be normal. So, too, with our businesses...change is normal. How we manage it is the trick.

Efficiency of leadership is a bit more difficult to see, though. Somehow, while we are clearing our desk of paperwork and while we take the time to look into our employees eyes when they are in our office, we also have to get more done in a day than most can in a week. This is our time management discussion. This is when we have to find a way to do everything only once, to multi task without losing focus, to make every minute count. How do we balance the need to move quickly without making those we lead feel rushed? How can we get more done in less time?

Well, some of this you are born with, or you are not. The ability to just think faster on your feet is somewhat rare.

But you also need courage. In fact, we should add that to the original list, shouldn't we...along with decisive? For many situations, to be efficient you simply have to make a decision and keep moving. Paralysis by analysis, as a friend used to call it, can cost you in many ways. Are you waiting for proof positive that your decision will be right? Unless you are a doctor saving lives, that probably isn't necessary! Get as much information as you can, set yourself some parameters and make a decision. You can always adjust as you go along.

Now, here is where taking more time can make you faster. If you take the time to genuinely understand your people, your customers, your products, then you can make these decisions on your feet much faster when the time comes. You'll find yourself feeling like you act on instinct, when in reality you're acting based on long, careful research. Knowing your product doesn't take that long. Knowing your employees and your customers is a major investment in time, but it will be worth it.

If you are new to a leadership role, I should mention that in every experience I've had myself, and with many that I've coached and mentored, it takes about two years to have a real rhythm in a management or leadership role. Yep. Two whole years. These days, that seems to some like an eternity! In a 45-year career, though, it's not really that much. It'll lead you eventually to long term thinking — without which, no matter what other traits you have, you cannot succeed as a leader.

Having said that, I'll add that the other place you have to keep up is with technology. My younger readers will be rolling their eyes. DUH! But many of us have lived through this transition. It's wonderful for helping your efficiency. The ability to create and store documents, and modify them later *(avoiding the "reinvention of the wheel")* is, by itself, an amazing time saver. But pay attention to the taxonomy. Look hard at how easily you can find things. Have a standard! I've been a huge proponent of the fullest use of technology since we first started using agency management systems! Below is a note I wrote to my staff back in 1995 or so about a computer upgrade. *(For those younger readers, if you don't know what carbon paper is, you can Google it.)*

### DOES ANYONE REMEMBER CARBON PAPER????

Remember the miracle of not having to type every single copy of the contract? Remember the smudging, ink all over your fingers, can't make a correction on the copy but wasn't it great to be able to (manually!) type the contract only once and get 2 or 3 or 4 copies? Then someone (XEROX?) had the idea that we could actually take a picture of the original contract and have as many copies as we wanted! And at a page a minute, no less! Then came the word processor, and the computer, and the fax, and the optical scanner, and bar coding, and pagers, and cellular phones, and AWAY WE WENT! Now isn't just so annoying when it takes three tries to get a fax through (instead of three days by U.S. Mail) or the laser printer is jammed and we have to change the paper so it takes 10 minutes to print a 45-page application? It is so hard to keep up sometimes. I type this E-mail once and it will go to 63 stations AT THE SAME TIME. Last week we began implementation [of a new system] on some of our workstations. Right now, it is in testing stages, and only a small percentage of us are using it. But it is the most advanced technology the insurance industry has to handle the overwhelming amount of information that we have to process. We get a new upgrade about every six months, and each time "the ink smudges" a bit and we have a few things to work out. But our system is far more advanced than the others, and much better than onion skin and carbon paper! Thank you for being patient with us as we work to provide you with the very best tools available to help you do your jobs efficiently and EFFECTIVELY.

My point here is that even if you are taking time, being patient, and thinking long term, you still have to think like a young whippersnapper when it comes to technology. Embrace it, use it, and don't pass the buck to an assistant for every little thing. This brings us back to the building analogy: don't you expect your home to have the most up to date wiring, plumbing and electronics? Or is the old VCR *(what's a VCR?...some may ask)* still flashing 12:00 at your house? As a leader, stay up to date. If you expect the staff to do it, you had better take the time yourself.

## *Patience*

We're building our analogies around houses, starting with the foundation. *But how can a house be patient?* Well, if built correctly you can paint it ugly colors and the house doesn't care, it will be patient with you about that. It will still provide shelter and comfort and will stand up when the wind blows. A house is patient when the children Crayola the walls or you neglect to wash it for years at a time. The longevity of a house, and its strength to stand the test of time, equate to patience.

And as leaders, we need patience on so many different levels. Ugly decisions get made sometimes — sometimes because we made a mistake and sometimes because that is what the company needs — a difficult, ugly decision. But the core, the foundation of the business, will survive. Some would say that ugly decisions are needed when the economy is bad and we have to lay people off. Often, layoffs are the result of bad management during the good times, when we were over indulgent. I have had half a dozen business owners tell me that they used tough economic times to "cut the dead wood" that they ought to have trimmed much sooner. Or, layoffs are because we are impatient, which is really my point. Our greatest asset is, or should be, our people. And when we are faced with expense reduction, everyone wants to try to hang on to the people. Sometimes, we do this for emotional reasons: "I really like Jane." or "We are a family." The better reason to keep people on board is because you were managing well to begin with, and there is a little reserve so you can be patient, knowing that when the economy turns around (it always does) you can use those folks to bring about recovery in your firm. You won't have to go find, hire and train anyone new. Note that this assumes you are up to date, and you aren't selling an obsolete product which won't survive anyway. Even when layoff or other "ugly" decisions really are the answer for the moment, your house will stand if founded in basic, long term strategy.

Sometimes, the temptation is to cancel a project before it has a chance to fully mature, or when there is a slump in production and you get into a short-term thinking mentality.

Consider that every product goes through slumps, and some are never even meant to make any money anyway. It takes considerable patience to decide if you really need to pull the plug or if you need to remember to look through your long-term glasses. For example, if a product defines your brand, and yet barely breaks even, is it worth the risk of anonymity? Maybe that product brings folks into your store, even if it's not your biggest money maker. Or maybe you have a project that helps ensure the longevity of your industry, or encourages young people to consider a career in your field, but it's costing a few dollars. [Remember: Don't keep pulling up the flowers to check the roots.]

Sometimes, we Crayola the walls. We add things we don't need or try things that don't work out. If we are patient with ourselves, and with our people, we can survive these little deviations to the plan. A little color is good, and some change is absolutely critical. It keeps the brain engaged to mix things up a bit and that is good for you as a leader and for your people. Now, don't implement change for change sake, just because you get bored! Pay attention to the ebb and flow of human nature, and you'll see that an adjustment here and there helps the human brain stay creative.

You've probably heard of the *Hawthorne Effect* and the lighting study that proved this. There was a company who was studying the lighting in the work area. With every change made productivity increased, whether the lighting got better or worse. There were lighting types that should have made it physically impossible for the employees to improve, but they did. In the end, it turned out to be more of a case of industrial psychology than the physiology of lighting needs! The employees were so excited that management cared enough about them to engage the study that they got more and more productive as it went along.

*Be patient. Stay the course. Trust your people, and create a culture of patience. It'll pay off — in the long run.*

## *Flexibility*

Engineers and physical therapists will associate with this analogy better than others. *Flexibility is the key to strength;* high rise buildings and slightly used up bodies need it to survive. There is a well-known parable about the flexible willow tree who survived the storm when the mighty oak snapped in two.

Houses are flexible, too. You can change a lot in a house without hurting its basic structure or strength. You can remodel, you can add new carpet or paint, you can make an addition or remove the old deck...and structurally, a house is built to withstand the pressures and forces of the ground underneath and the environment above.

Those pressures and forces are pushing on you, too, as a leader. You have forces from below and all around you asking for your time, your opinion, and your resources. If you are feeling the strain, you may need to flex!

Flexibility takes practice. Spend some time checking this point occasionally. How often do you look at situations or staff and list options for solving a problem? Have you fallen into the mode of doing everything by the book? Are you barking out orders or asking your folks to help solve the project and bring you three options? Take a big, deep breath before you answer; remember how important it is to keep your brain energized! Stress causes that barking, by the way, and breathing well helps you handle it. We are learning more all the time, but one neuroscientist says that when you're taking slow, deep breaths, your ancient brain knows you're not in danger. Why? Because you usually don't take slow breaths when you're running from a tiger.*

Worst of all, are you looking at your firm or situation from a single-issue point of view? Long term, strategic thinking allows you to be flexible in two ways. First, you know the larger mission of your firm. Mission is never just "making a profit," is it? How many times have you seen a plaque on the wall with that? Mission has a bigger purpose; money is just one of the means to get you there. The second thing long range planning gives you is a sense of

*[SQ21, Cindy Wigglesworth]

the various options you'll have in getting to your mission, because you'll see the bigger picture.

Don't let the long-range plan trap you, though. You do need to check it and adjust sometimes. You'll need to review and adapt, just as a house needs an occasional power wash to prep and re-paint. This is where flexibility comes in as well. The building blocks on your pillars occasionally need replacing. Once those KPIs are met, they become part of operations if it's an ongoing process. Situations change so quickly that most professional planning consultants will say 18 months to three years is as far out as we can go. It used to be five years! Now, we just have a brief concept of five or ten years out.

Flexibility with staff is urgent, always. You may think that with an odd job market *(such as the pandemic of 2020)* new hires are easy pickings and you don't think you have to take great care with the folks you have. This is wrong on many counts, but to name two: unless it's a true RIF — reduction in force — the best employees don't get laid off during recessions, usually. The marginal ones do. But more importantly, the training you have to do when you lose a great employee, and the institutional knowledge they carry away with them *(that you lose)* all costs you more than you may think. Even when times are tough, don't pull back on employee benefits if you can help it. Give up executive perks; those are easy to get back later. Keep all the fun stuff in place too, the soft cost type things like birthday celebrations and team retreats that don't hurt the bottom line but make people glad to get up and come to the office.

*One last point. Flexibility does not equate to speed.* Take just one yoga class and you'll see what I mean. The key to flexibility is long, slow, deep stretching. Just as it can take years to master a yoga pose, it takes long, thoughtful, careful engineering for a building or house or a business to be flexible. So, while it's tempting to define our quick reactions to changing environments or speed to market as flexibility, it's really not. Speed is important, but that is a topic for later!

## *Functionality*

*Houses can be highly functional* right from the start; they are usually pre-wired for phone, Internet, cable TV, security and so on. Some have in wall vacuum systems, or built-ins like desks or book shelves. The kitchens have double sinks as do the bathrooms, even the ones on the pool deck! Flow of the layout is a serious consideration in the planning.

Most great leaders are pre-wired for it. They were born with some kink in the brain that makes them able to do the things that are required to bring about great change, even if that change is in a small realm. Everyone can be a leader, just as every house can be retrofit for cable TV or in wall vacuums. But when it's a part of the natural ability of the person, it just comes easier.

There is an amazing book called *Soar with Your Strengths* that discusses the natural abilities of people. This book focused on the American school system, but it is easily transferable to all aspects of life. Similarly, First, Break All the Rules has the same discussion about natural talent in the workplace. The DiSC profile is popular and one of my favorites for assessing natural tendencies. It's worthwhile to explore these. Can you identify your own natural talents? It's not as easy as it seems. Talents are different from knowledge or strengths. Talents have been with you since childhood. Think about this. Make a list. And eventually, have this discussion with your crew. Have time to assess each year if everyone is in their most productive and effective role. All you have to do is ask; they'll tell you.

## *Emotionally Balanced*

You know, it's hard to imagine an *emotional house* — but the sanest thing I ever heard of in living spaces was the split plan! Now, I don't have kids, but if I did that type of house would be required. It's not the kids; it's the balance that such a plan provides. You know about Maslow's pyramid and topics such as nourishment and rest. The emotional balance that a great leader needs is pretty important, since you can't be flying off the handle if you want to positively influence people. Emotional balance is actually a lot of work to create. It probably comes naturally at birth, but we stomp out the instinct for play and for rest as we get further into our careers.

The best scenario is when work IS play, when work feels restful, and when the way we make our living is the thing that comforts us the most. Even when you are one of the lucky ones who feel this way about their career, though, there are times when things can get out of balance. In those times, it helps to have a proven method to bring yourself back to center. People are counting on you. Self-care does not come natural to some of us. Some see it as selfish. Self-care is not selfish. In fact, it's the most loving thing we can do for others, because it helps us to be at our best when we are together. We tend to sacrifice for the good of the cause, and then when we are no longer able to function, the entire cause could be sacrificed. Airline attendants have been saying for years that we should put our own oxygen mask on first, and then assist others. But how do we do that and not feel the guilt and pull of the "job?"

First, getting enough rest is so basic and so overlooked. Our culture is shameful about this. Many other cultures allow long afternoon breaks. We give 15 minutes. We work nine- and ten-hour days, and count folks lucky to get to go to lunch for an hour. Our zeal for the bottom line is short term. The loss of intellectual property and institutional knowledge when we have serious, stress induced illness due to over-work is quite costly to the company. And our employees have important knowledge we lose too when we drive them away or ask them to forgo rest for the sake of the bottom line. We take pride in statements like "I haven't taken a vacation in years!" Shame on you! This is at our own long-term peril. It's great to be proud of your work, and to put in the hours because you are dedicated and loyal. At some point, though, burn out is inevitable if you don't pay attention.

Here's the thing about rest, and vacations, and long lunches. We must work both sides of the brain for it to function best. Creativity is sparked with and by new experiences. We are not whole if we only work. The time we spend not working is when our brain can rejuvenate on one side and grow on the other. A loose analogy is the time required to rest between weight lifting sessions in order for the muscle to repair itself. Those tiny tears we make in the muscle while lifting repair themselves with new tissue which makes the muscle larger. Does your brain ever get that chance?

Going back to the analogy of the house — would a house function best if it was one big space, one room, one purpose? Of course not. Otherwise that is how we would still build them. Centuries ago, we sought only shelter, and one room served us well. Now, we know that the house can allow us so many more pleasures and functions! Your brain *(and heart)* needs time to do more than work; it's not serving you best if you treat it as a single function machine.

Rest doesn't just mean sleep! It means time spent on other things, other people. When I teach sales, I talk about networking with a variety of groups: business, philanthropic, industry, and hobby. My sales students are always surprised that I require them to join a hobby group. Some don't even know how to find one. But that creative time, working on the other side of their brain when the pressure is not about productivity can spark more innovation that any other type of function.

Don't forget sleep. Studies have proven how valuable it is to brain function, and the amount needed for each person varies. Know your biorhythms. It's not selfish to get appropriate rest. Just keep telling yourself you'll be more useful to those who count on you if you take care of yourself properly. There are only so many hours in a day, and sometimes the only way to get your rest is to say "No" or "maybe later" to someone's request. This is hard, especially for us "A" types who would take on the world. But do it anyway. Be brave...and sleep.

### *Empathetic*

*Empathetic houses are real.* Office buildings have these qualities too, and it's not Star Trek. The lights come on when you walk into the room, heat and air settings are pre-programmed, security systems sense your presence...the house anticipates your needs and knows what to do for you.

A great leader is empathetic too. Employees have the tools they need to do the job, usually without asking for them. Managers know how the job is done, and can provide guidance to the employee by anticipating their needs. Instructions are clear, deadlines are firm, and the place hums with productivity.

A lot can get in the way of that empathy, though. While a great manager doesn't have to be the best at the type of work being done (the best managers aren't the best players in sports, either) they do have to completely understand the mechanics of the job. If they don't, for example if they were actually bad at those tasks and were promoted for the wrong reasons, or if they didn't get proper training themselves, they won't be able to be empathic managers.

And empathy is an emotion, too. Long gone are the days where we didn't talk about personal issues at work; where we "left work at the door" when we got home and never the twain should meet. Technology being what it is — it's all connected now. We talk less about work/life balance and more about work life blend. We work from home and we pay bills on line from the office. It's more productive. But it also means that it's messier. Some managers hate that! They would rather have a hard line in the sand about the use of time at the office. But, sorry to be the messenger here, managing time is just the lazy way out. Productivity measurements are much more difficult than time measurements. Time cards and punch clocks are going to go the way of the buggy whip in many industries. The 2020 pandemic has proven that working from home works!

That means at least a little thought has to be put into the problems and joys of the employees personal and home life, without interfering or becoming inappropriate. Also, not easy! But the consideration given, when life is tough for an employee, is paid back ten-fold when they come back 100%. And you can't buy the loyalty that comes when you allow folks the time to take care of things at home.

Over nearly three decades I've conducted hundreds of personality profiles of varying types. In almost every class at least one person says: "Do I answer this as if I am at work, or at home?" My answer, always with a smile, is "Hmmm. Are you schizophrenic?" Usually this draws a laugh and I explain that while we may adjust our behavior at work, who we are, at our core, doesn't change. The idea is that if we can learn to be ourselves completely at work, we'll be more successful. Sometimes that means leaving one industry, where our personality and natural talents don't match, and going to a new one.

Great leaders see this God given talent, the natural personality of their people, and they are empathic to it. They place people in jobs very carefully, matching the person's talent to the vision of the firm and the duties of the particular position. There are many aids to this, such as ZeroRisk®, DiSC, Caliper, Omnia and the like. These are simply tools, one of many factors in such decisions. The book *First, Break All the Rules* has a terrific discussion of the Gallup Poll study supporting the concepts.

*Consider the word empathy, and its varying meanings, as it relates to you, the leader.*

## Talent

*It takes a considerable amount of talent to build a house.* Using our foundation analogy, you can think about how much talent it takes just to get that first part right. Architects, engineers, planners, machine operators, carpenters, masons...all are a part of that first important step. And there's no excuse for discounting the talent to do what most would call the lesser work. If the person running the bulldozer doesn't get it right, the project can grind to a fast halt; or worse yet, the foundation can fail later.

Foundations are a great example too of Stephen Covey's wisdom to "begin with the end in mind." If we plan the foundation to support ten stories, we can't change our mind later and make the building 20 stories tall without major, costly adjustments.

The same is true with talent. When hiring, buy the best talent you can possibly afford knowing where you want the firm to be in five or ten years. Going cheap on talent now is a costly mistake when you want to move forward later. This is a circular argument, of course, and brings us back to planning and strategy.

*First, Break All the Rules* is, in my opinion, one of the best management texts to be written in years. Besides being born of a scientific study, proving its theories, it's a highly practical volume. The discussion of talent versus experience and education is worth a quick look. When you are hiring, you should try to see if the job you want to fill is a match to the prospect's natural desires and tendencies. Is this the thing they were born to do? While every day of every job isn't ever going to match that description, you need that sense of passion and desire from the candidate to make the most of the money you spend.

For example, if you have two candidates that you like, one having been in the business for 20 years and the other for only five, how do you know if you can take the risk of the younger (maybe less costly) candidate? The answer lies in their natural innate talent and passion for your business. If the person with 20 years has been working in the industry begrudgingly, because they 'fell into' the first job and never got out, you probably want to pass. They may have "20 years in" but it may just be the first year, 20 times! Of course, if they have 20 years of talent, passion and a natural instinct for your business at hand, it's worth paying more! The same questions apply to the five-year candidate. They may be worth the risk if you can determine their level of raw talent and then direct them to your methods.

Taking care with human resource laws surrounding interviews, you'll want to ask them very specific questions, with less focus on how they do things and more about why they are in the industry.

One rare caveat: just because someone has a talent to do something it doesn't mean they like doing it. While rare, sometimes it happens. My personal example is in golf. I took lessons and played for a very short time, and was told again and again I was a natural. But at that time in my life I simply wasn't enjoying the game; despite the "potential" I seemed to have. Sometimes, you'll run into that situation, where a person has 20 years doing something that they have a natural talent to do, but just plain don't like it. The same probing in an interview can reveal this.

Take a minute to look at your entire staff this way. Who is joyful at work and who isn't? Who's having fun? Why? If you could move folks around to take more advantage of the natural talents, why not do it?

Remember that talents must be nurtured. No matter how natural you are at something, if you don't practice, you'll get rusty. So, take time to practice, get education, and do more of what you love. Same goes for your employees! It can only make you better!

## *Disciplined*

*A disciplined house has a lot of parallels for our topic.* You could say that a disciplined house stays square *(retains shape),* the foundation doesn't settle, the plumbing is consistent, the wiring is sound, etc...all over the course of time. It's great when the house is new, and everything works well. But is the house "disciplined" enough that in five, 10, 20 years it still all works?

Leadership principles are like that. You stick to them, and succeed, or you meander and the house falls down. Staying firm in your values, visions and resolve, once you have very carefully defined what those are, is important. Now, to regress just for a minute: you can't stay firm in your visions if you haven't planned them carefully and documented them.

You have to be who you are, all the time...or seriously, see a therapist. That's a great self-care activity too! Too many people try to be one person at work and another at home, as if the person they already are isn't good enough for one place or the other. It's the cause of a lot of heartache and stress. So, make a decision about the values you want to uphold and commit. Get a coach to hold you accountable, if you need that. It will make life easier.

Your actions, behavior and attitudes are under scrutiny every single day. Someone is always watching: employees, friends, children, bosses, peers, or neighbors. Your mom might have gotten away with saying, "Do as I say, not as I do" but even when she said it, she knew it was a flimsy argument! So, consistent behavior, which takes incredible discipline to employ, is important. You are influencing the actions of others whether you know it or not.

It's not about you. For example, if you want to "stay square" you'll need to be able to act your values even on days when you don't feel like it. If you've professed to be the boss with the open door all the time, then one day the door is closed all day long, staff will make up whatever stories make sense to explain it. This can spiral into a lot of distracting gossip. So, if you need a day to hibernate, do it at home.

Or, *(the bricks vs. clicks discussion notwithstanding)* perhaps you've decided attendance is critical at your workplace, and you reward consistent attendance and praise those who miss the least days, and so on. That means you also need to make the effort to be in the office every day.

You get the point. Your discipline about how you handle your job is reflecting back on everyone. Your discipline about your values reflects back upon you!

This affects you in the long run, because if you don't personally show discipline in the small things, no one will believe you for the big ones. The house will crumble. So, when you profess yourself, your own values, your personal mission, use caution. Be sure you can live up to your own standards.

## *Persistence*

*How is a house persistent?* Well, in a storm, you want that door to stay shut no matter how hard the wind blows. You want the windows to persist in hard rain. You want the wind to buffet the roof and not get in. That's persistency. One song says something about getting up one more time than you fall down...that's another way to look at it. In sales classes we teach to make just one more call, no matter how many times you've been turned down.

In leadership, though, persistence can be thought of as having to do with values. It's not consistency of process but more about sticking to your guns despite what's happening around you. As leaders, we need to be persistent in our pursuit of integrity, values, long term goals, and advocacy for our people. We have to be the ones who don't give up in tough times, and who act out the example of positive, persistent optimism in tough times. There is always talk about the economy being the problem. It was the conversation in 2009 when I opened my consulting practice and in 2020 when we started compiling this book. But we must persist. And next time, when we're high on the hog, maybe we'll save a little more and spend a little less corporately, too. The economy is an easy excuse and a glaring reminder that everything cycles. So, if we can level it all out a bit, by being persistent to our values and goals whether we're in an up or down, good or bad, easy or hard time in our industry, economy, or business/company, it won't be so hard next time. And, sometimes the crisis tries to define us — don't let it. Keep the wind out, and the rain at bay. This is not easy, and it's not going to happen by chance. It takes careful thought no matter what the season to be prepared for the storm. And you might not be able to do it alone. But you can do it.

Henry Ford said: "In good times, people do business with friends. In bad times, people do business with friends. Make friends."

## Consistency

*Consistency in a house is very important to its long-term functionality.* If standards of building elements aren't used, it wreaks havoc on the building process and on future repairs. For example, if non-standard windows and doors are used, then you must make everything one at a time, such as in a custom build. While custom homes are popular, even those homes generally use standard sizes of windows and doors. This way, when a window breaks later it is easier and more affordable to repair. And, every house must use standard electrical items and plumbing fixtures in order to be functional. If the flow of electricity isn't consistent, you could blow the breaker...or worse.

So must the work product be consistent. If the roofer isn't consistent in his work style from day to day, that roof will leak.

Consistency in our leaders helps with functionality in the workplace, too. If you as a leader are consistent in the application of your values, and fair in the use of your authority, your followers will be consistent in their work product as well.

But if you are "the good guy" one day and "the bad boss" the next, your employees won't be able to focus on the task at hand. They'll always be wondering what is next, and fear follows. This is a terrible environment in which to work no matter how talented the staff may be. Inconsistent application of values can wreak havoc on the workforce and your firm's productivity. This issue is often indicative of a leader who hasn't yet defined his or her own values, and probably hasn't done the visionary "who are we" exercise for the firm, either. Not knowing the "who" leads to many problems with the what, why and how.

Inconsistency in work process is also an issue in so many ways. When standards are either not made or not enforced, your product or service will present poorly to the buyer. The buyer may expect something other than what they receive. This can lead to a range of problems: simple dissatisfaction, outright upset or disgust which leads to bad press and loss of reputation, or even errors and omissions and professional liability issues. The most common problem in professional liability is not lack of standards; it's the lack of application of those standards. Translation: *inconsistency.*

This creates a vicious circle for the staff, too. Some-times, we jump up and down about the needs for use of standards. We have meetings and teleconferences and create checklists and workflow grinds to a halt. Then, after a while, when everyone is exhausted, we back off and in the sheer relief that comes with the break, everyone gets a little loose.

Instead, consider a measured, practiced, consistent application of the processes that are truly critical: documentation of the standard of work, communication about the reasons and priorities and an even flow of measurement, meetings and other functions that enforce and uphold the practices you want employed. Eat the elephant one bite at a time, until the process is simply second nature. Make this a part of the overall strategic plan, and create simple, time-based checkpoints for everyone. Once implemented, try to keep the process the same for a few years, so you can see trend lines.

In addition, one last piece of advice: be sure you are consistently applying these standards to yourself as a leader. Practice what you preach. Never mind that this will create trust in your staff and peers, which it will, but know that you'll actually feel better and more centered if you do.

The best part about documenting processes isn't the actual document. The conversations are where the real magic happens.

Here are a few of the documents and processes that you may need:

## Business Documents Checklist

- o  Business Plan
- o  Strategy
- o  Plan on a Page Poster
- o  Quarterly Strategic Reporting Forms
- o  Tactical Plan for Each KPI *(Key Performance Indicator)*
- o  Succession Plan
- o  Financial Statements
- o  HR Manual
- o  Disciplinary Forms
- o  Performance Review Forms
- o  Job Descriptions
- o  Key Performance Indicators
- o  Organization Chart
- o  Specific Technical Procedures Manual(s)
- o  Marketing Messages
- o  Press Kit
- o  Operational Agreement
- o  Bylaws
- o  Standard NDA *(Non-Disclosure Agreement)*
- o  Employment Agreement
- o  Non-Piracy Agreement
- o  Founders Agreement
- o  IP Agreements *(Intellectual Property)*
- o  Online Privacy Agreement

## *Resourceful*

*Leaders need to be resourceful in ways that many would not even realize.* Their resourcefulness is in fact generally not noticed until it is gone. Leaders are the type, usually, who just get it done, and drawing on the many resources they have gathered up without making a lot of fanfare about how they did it. They will know where something is kept, how to do it, who to ask, what time the event is — because they have an ability to pay attention, retain the information, and are unafraid to answer questions not asked directly of them. Sounds a little like most moms, too!

In the same way living rooms become multi-function rooms used for fellowship, dining, fort-building by kids, school project rooms, game rooms, movie night and so on, a leader's "multi-function" is often the fact that they literally become the resource. Generally, too, this leadership trait will cross departments, companies and industries. The talent will show itself in the office, at home, at church, etc.

When asked "How do you do that?" the leader won't always know. Sometimes, this is a leadership trait that is inborn more than learned. And so just as a living room is a room no matter what function it's taking on at any given moment, a leader is a leader whether or not they hold a corresponding title at work, or if they are just being who they are at home or at church.

If you are a leader who doesn't feel you have this trait, you're probably just not drawing it out. You can become more resourceful if you are simply willing to open up a bit. For the most part, this trait is honed by listening more and being willing to ask a lot of questions. It comes with experience and coaching, too.

## *Fair*

*How is a house fair??* What correlation could we possibly make here? Well, houses are color blind, gender neutral and don't care how pretty you are. They don't worry about your background, or the amount of money you donate to charity. Houses just perform for you, protecting you from the elements and allowing you to rest and recharge.

Leaders should be just as fair. Everyone doesn't get a trophy...but everyone should get a chance. Anyway, fairness has many faces. Sometimes, in order to do what you have to do to keep the ship afloat, your decisions will feel "unfair" to some of your employees or vendors. But in the end, you are the one who has to convince those folks that you are being fair to all by making the decisions.

Just be sure that you're properly motivated, and that you are taking into consideration everyone's stake in the game, and that you've explored every opportunity to do what you need to do for the sake of the organization before you make a final choice. Get lots of opinions from folks who are affected. The hardest part here is to talk to several folks without actually committing to one course of action before you get all the information. We get excited...and we say YES, I LIKE IT...and someone assumes that you are going to do it their way. So, take a breath and say, "I like it; I'll add it to the list of possibilities." That keeps everyone on the same page.

Sometimes, the roof leaks. When it does, it leaks on everyone in the house/room, no matter who they are. When you have to make the tough decisions, please be sure you're evaluating performance, not likeability. As humans, we can't help that tendency, but as leaders we can destroy all credibility when we are "more fair" to our friends or golfing buddies without sufficient corresponding merit.

It's not always as simple as wondering if you can sleep at night or whether you can look at yourself in the mirror afterward...but that's a great start.

## *Ethical*

*Most folks wouldn't think of ethics as something a house can emulate.* We are comparing houses to leadership traits, because of the philosophy here at Sapphire Enterprises that the key to all good leadership is a strong foundation. And houses do indeed have something to share regarding ethics. A well-built house is well built everywhere, even when you can't see it. Finishing details do not cover up poor work; the structure and wiring and plumbing and everything underneath have the same high quality as the pretty wallpaper or nice fixtures.

This is as it should be with ethical leadership. If we talk the talk, but we are rotten underneath with a hidden agenda, we aren't truly leaders. Is it all just lip service, or do we mean it? One quick way to find out about yourself is this: how many times have you passed someone in the hall at the office and asked "How are you?" and actually stopped to listen to the answer? It's a small detail, but it says a lot about whether your words and your intentions are aligned. It's perfectly fine to greet someone with "Hey" or "Good Morning" and not ask how they are. But to ask and then keep walking is a small insult that adds up over time.

When we are building relationships, which is the only path to great leadership, we have to actually care about the person involved. This cannot be faked. If you can't really bring yourself to care, with true emotion, about the people involved in your work or project, you are probably doing the wrong work!

Note that I've not said you have to like everyone. Liking someone and caring about their welfare are two different things. And caring only about their productivity is not the same either. That's a motivation for selfish reasons. Do you actually care underneath it all about the person? If you do, and you try to align their talents with the job they have to do for you, everyone will win. You'll have better productivity because you have a happier, more fulfilled employee!

There are rules about how involved you can get in an employee's personal life. I'm not suggesting we violate those, of course, but it doesn't preclude us from stopping and listening to the answer when we ask the question "How are you?" I learned this from a wonderful boss once, during a particularly bad time in my personal life. He came to my office one evening and asked "How is it going?" I answered with details about the departments I was managing, and the productivity of my staff. He listened, but then he asked again: "No, Lisa" he said, "How are YOU?" It was a profound moment of leadership for him, and I'll never forget it. He didn't need to do anything for me; just knowing he cared enough to ask, and listen, made a world of difference to me. Thanks, Sam.

The original version of this chapter was an article that I penned on Christmas Eve. So, I'll end on a note of personal privilege. If you want to say Merry Christmas, please say it. If you prefer Happy Hanukkah, then you should respond accordingly. If you like Kwanza, then that's a good response to my "Merry Christmas," too. I truly believe that if we all have our own greeting and the response by others was in their own method, unashamed, we'd open the doors of understanding and grace that we are seeking in the seasons we celebrate.

## *Strength*

*There are a couple of analogies I can draw to strength.* First, I thank God for a strong house. We have survived a couple of rare winter freezes in the DFW area, and while this house is old, it is good shelter! Sometimes, you just have to appreciate the basics.

Secondly, as I wrote a section years ago for my blog, we were just a day away from one of the biggest events in Arlington history: the Superbowl, a testament to a team's physical, emotional and cultural strength if there ever was one.

Leaders, like houses and sports teams, must hold up to the various weather conditions of life. They must provide the basic necessity of safety, security, shelter for their staff no matter what is going on around them.

Sometimes, the threat is from within. Cultures in organizations define so much about the success of the business. Leaders who don't lead culturally miss a chance to shape and teach their people about the bigger picture. This is loosely connected to the "teach a man to fish" story.

If a leader can build a strong culture of safety and security in all types of weather, the staff will know what to do no matter what the circumstances. They will be equipped to handle the heat waves and the cold snaps. When it's hot, and we're doing well, and the product is flying out the doors, we can get lazy. In the cold times, when we can't give the product away, we can get defensive. But if we are secure in our culture and strong in our purpose, we don't have to fall apart in those ways. If we assume the best in ourselves and our teammates, we can weather all the storms. This all comes from the example of the leaders!

Part of building the strong foundation is building the strong, positive culture. It sets the stage for how challenges are handled for all time. If you find that your culture has weakened, it can take years to repair, just as correcting a shifting foundation is a major endeavor. Maybe you've been so busy trying to keep your customers you forgot about your employees. Perhaps instead of looking for new sources of revenue you've spent all your time cutting operational expenses. Have you lost sight of the internal while managing the external?

Therefore, it is in your best interest to see to the culture of your shop daily. Are we living the values we profess on the poster on the wall? Pay attention. Dare I say it — eat in the lunchroom with the brown bag staff once in a while. Listen carefully to the stories of their lives. Hire well; hire to your culture.

Of course, this requires that you know the definition of the culture of your organization; and that you can articulate what it is and how it should feel. Do you have a culture of fun, play, excitement? Seriousness in purpose? Happiness in work? Or is it a culture of gossip and finger pointing? Clock punching and back stabbing? No one intends this to happen, of course. But it does, and it's a silent killer just like the deep freeze.

Get help if you need it, because once the culture cracks, the wind can howl right in. The whole building can crumble. But if the culture is sound, the warmth can build and spread and grow – and your customers will feel it all around them. Most customers will be drawn to that warmth!

## *Holistic*

*Leaders and houses can strive to be holistic.* Dictionary.com defines *holistic* as: "the theory that whole entities, as the fundamental components of reality, having an existence other than as the mere sum of their parts."

I like to think of this more simply, as in "the bigger picture." Or, you could consider it as embracing the bigger flow of things, so that as a leader you aren't making decisions in a vacuum.

When we bought our house, one consideration was that we knew we'd have regular guests, and sometimes long-term guests. This creates the need for a house with a great overall flow, for entertaining, but separateness, for the longer-term situations. And, we needed a little extra space. We had to look past the smaller details to be sure the long-term use would still work. And, the sum of the parts had to work together well. We are blessed; we found that house. And we're always sharing it.

As leaders, we need to look beyond the parts and pieces sometimes and be sure we see the effect we are having on the whole place. Will our decision today have a ripple effect tomorrow? Are others going to be affected by the moves we make? Will a termination in one department have impact on another? How will the decisions be viewed both internally and externally? Have we considered upcoming changes in our industry? Our company? Our personal lives? How will those things impact the decisions we make today? Be sure the puzzle pieces fit.

A major part of this process needs to be to take a minute and think — holistically! In many of my articles and keynotes

I talk about slowing down to think. This is what gives you time to look over the top of your desk and study carefully the impact of your decisions. Some decisions have to be made quickly, but that doesn't mean all the proper preparation can't be in place so that you can make a good decision in a short time.   This is why foundations are so important. If you have all the fundamental, foundational information and structures in place, if data flow is continuous and well managed, if you are getting the right updates and keeping a close tab on things, you can move much more quickly when it is truly needed.

However, every decision won't make or break the company if you pause to think. We are simply so trained to think that way now that we rush through things even when it is not needed.   We say things like "I don't have time for a time management class." I've heard that one a lot!

◆

## *Fearless*

*Courage is an important part of being a great leader.* It is, despite the title of this chapter, not the absence of fear. Courage is feeling the fear and doing it anyway. You may appear fearless to your charges, but most of us still have the fear, and do what we need to do despite that feeling. In fact, having a little fear is healthy and keeps us alive! There isn't an exact parallel, but I see the idea of "fearlessness" in a house as that older home that has a few nicks and scratches and even a hole or two in the wall or a few shingles off the roof, but it still holds up in a storm.

No one is perfect. And we all feel fear. When we handle that fear appropriately, as great leaders do, we can acknowledge it and move forward anyway. Your crew will be looking for your reaction with things aren't going as planned. They want your guidance. If you model the good behaviors, like pausing to think, evaluating the situation, following the plans that were made for these eventualities, holding your head high when others aren't supportive, and so on, they will learn from you.

You actually should feel just a little bit uncomfortable all the time. If we are too settled and too comfortable, we probably aren't taking enough risks. Remember though: pruning the plant isn't the same as pulling it up anxiously to check to see how the roots are doing. Trim, prune, fertilize, water, pull off the invasive bugs or weeds....But let your plans grow even if you feel uncomfortable.

This isn't about you. Knowing how far you can go with the discomfort is important too. Know yourself, and your limits, and delegate, delegate, delegate!

## Decisive

The plumbing in a house knows exactly what to do. The electricity doesn't try to be the plumbing, and the foundations doesn't try to do the work of the roof.

*Your job as the leaders, is to make great decisions.* It's not your job to figure out HOW we do things. It's not your job to analyze the details. It's not your job to lay out the tactical plan. Those jobs belong to your crew. Your work is in strategy, and making the decisions that take us where we need to go.

We need decisive leaders, who can see and execute the work as planned without constant deviations. It's OK if you need to take a reasonable about of time to evaluate and think and analyze, just don't miss the opportunity because you can't make a decision. Everyone is frozen until you say "go!" So, having trust in your people is critical, too. Have trust that they can do that analysis, make those tactical processes, and figure out the details while you move on to the next long-term strategic decision. [See more in SECTION THREE — THE CREW]

## *Approachable*

*What makes a house approachable, giving it the "curb appeal" that realtors like to discuss?* It's the finish work inside and out, and the landscaping and exterior design, colors and details that make a house look like one you'd want to see, right? Bosses need to be approachable too, so that their crew is willing to tell them what's happening in the shop, and no be afraid to share when there is a problem.

One of the best ways to do this is to get out of your office. First, get out of your office within your office building or space. If you're virtual, it means visiting with folks on subjects not about work. It's harder to do, but the 2020 pandemic taught us a lot about team building virtually. You can find a lot of information if you look.

But for the in-person office, just walking around *(remember the old 'Management By Walking Around' days?)* and getting caught making the coffee, or taking lunch in the break room sometimes, can be pretty effective for this. It's not hard, you just have to remember to do it. Be seen in the Friday casual look sometimes. Brown bag the lunch. Share pictures of your family gathers once in a while, or hang your softball trophy on the wall in your office. Just be human.

Sometimes, it means getting out of the office with your team. It is hard to keep your perspective on the world, your community and your industry if you don't take time to see what is out there. You have people for this, of course, that are great sales folks and can man the booth at conferences. Imagine what you'll earn about them when you travel with them! And who might you meet that will be a great future employee? You can't do this often, of course, but you'll be a better leader if you do plan it occasionally. This isn't just about sales, or networking, or even education opportunities, although all of these are natural outcroppings of the meetings you might choose to attend if you decide to get a fresh perspective. It's also about seeing the industry through the eyes of others, whether in a group or just having lunch with someone who works in a different part of the industry you're in or outside the business entirely.

[There are bosses who can be approached and mean bosses who are judgmental. Ask me how communication training can help.]

## *Focused*

The turn of the year, whether by the calendar or fiscally, is a time when we start to lose it: focus. The reality of the new year hits. All our good intentions are fading fast. Busy is starting to overwhelm productivity. Your team is running hard, keeping up, doing great and the bigger goals are slipping away as the churning of your efforts in the minutia take over. What to do to get back on track?

If you're a house, one of the most important, and dangerous, items to keep in focus is the electricity. That is an amazing invention that can also kill you! If you're an electrician, you know all the steps and processes to be sure you don't get hurt. And as a homeowner, you want that electrical system to be installed correctly, and you want the safeguards in place so that there aren't accidents. The same focus, and prevention, are needed as a great leader.

First of all, just keep your focus. Don't get so overwhelmed by the multitude of choices *(or voices)* that you forget your mission. We have so many choices now about many things; even toothpaste has hundreds of brands! In our work, there are even more choices, but none more important than how we behave with our colleagues. We have the ability to be many things to many people. This is true both individually and for the collective 'we.'

As a leader, you have the responsibility to focus on many layers; but most importantly, maintain your own focus. If you are not modeling the best behavior here, how can others learn from you? When a staff member is speaking, are you really listening? Or are you trying to multi-task? Do you interrupt them to take a phone call? (Rude!) Is one eye on your email? Technically, in terms of brain function, we cannot multi-task. Inside our head we are actually bouncing from one thing back to the other over and over again. By doing this, our brain is up to 40% less effective, causing us to make more mistakes and potentially hurt someone's feelings.

Active listening may be one of the most difficult disciplines we have to practice. One simple but obvious idea: you need to actually look at your employee and really focus on them. Pick your head up from the desk and put the phone, paper, or other distractions down. Simply look at them while they are speaking. Amazingly, this can be really difficult. For example, do you have a notification bell on your email, ringing every time there is a new message? Turn it off! You might even minimize all the screens on your computer to reduce further distraction.

Next, clear a space across your desk *(if applicable)* so that there is no implied barrier between the two of you. Close up files and move them aside. The body language you employ can also help; lean in and focus. Nod, smile, and gesture!

You can also use verbal cues to let the person know you are engaged in the conversation. "Oh?" and "Uh, huh?" are two of my favorite ways to get a person to keep talking; I learned this from my friend Bill. Asking questions can also keep you focused as well as commenting on various aspects of the conversation, such as, "Wow, I bet that was hard to do!" or, "Great idea!" as you go along in the conversation.

This may seem rudimentary, but the most basic and important things we do are often the ones that get lost in the hurriedness of life. Unfortunately, we tend to ignore the polishing of these basic skills which are assumed to be done naturally. We are born knowing how to hear but not how to listen; this takes skill and practice. But this isn't the only focus you need.

What about the focus on your own set of needs, your own training, and your own time to think and process? Have you scheduled your own training time, your rest, and your time to think? Do you allow such time for your employees? In fact, do you insist upon them taking that time?

You also have responsibility to focus your team. Helping them keep their eye on the ball takes a great deal of effort and requires several steps.

By reading this book and building a *Strategy*, you're doing what must be done to have an up-to-date mission statement, then create language around that mission that empowers your internal code. Standardize everything to the values and mission you develop. Don't just brand your product; brand your mission. Virtually everything you do — internal documents, external news items, meeting agendas — can be organized or communicated around those concepts. This helps the ability to focus come very naturally, no longer requiring staff to listen to pontifications about the methodology; it also helps create a habit. Even accountability is enhanced because everyone will know what direction they are going all the time.

The second lesson is to take care of each other. Vigorously protect those you lead, and help them not to damage themselves. You may be empowering them by giving them all the rope they need to hang themselves, but never, ever let the trap door open below them. Don't let them work so hard they forget other priorities such as family and rest because no one wins when they are burned out.

Most generally, your best employees need most of your attention. We have the bad habit of spending more time on our marginal employees, hoping we can fix them. Unfortunately, this means we don't have time to develop the ones that actually deserve our time. Since we often allow the marginal employees to continue in their position way too long, we actually punish the "good ones" who end up carrying more than their share of the load. Because they are the good ones, they will continue to shoulder the load until they have deprived themselves of rest and refreshment; they may even burn out, which manifests in many forms: giving up, becoming ill due to lack of rest, or developing an attitude that suffers.

With this in mind, keep track of the time you spend with each employee, which will keep you from falling into a trap. It is fine to spend time trying to bring poor employees into the fold with training, attention, or even trying different assignments, but be sure the ratios are right.

Help them stay focused on the bigger mission. Others may try pulling them away from the task, but don't allow it. Be sure you are aware of all the distractions that are in the way of the people you lead, even if this means eliminating or giving new life to processes that are old or unnecessary; there may be stale procedures that are just, "the way we have always done it." These can easily rob you of efficiency and effectiveness.

Technology can have this effect as well. If all you have is a hammer, everything will look like a nail. Be sure your systems are current. This is difficult with the changes that come so fast, but the old rule of driving all work down to the lowest, cost-effective solution still stands. Similarly, if you have someone doing work that can be automated (or delegated), you have inefficiency. This does more than affect the bottom-line. Your staff eventually will be demoralized when they see the impact on their day simply because you won't make the investment in the right tools.

Another way to help keep folks focused is to reward the right behavior the right way. Remember that most folks want to do a great job, and you reward them by allowing them to do so when you provide the proper tools and the proper focus from you.

## *Visionary*

A house looks to family's future in design, shape, and size. *When someone builds or buys a house, or office building, there is usually strong consideration toward the future.* A leader must be like this.

Being a visionary is both first and last in terms of priority; it's where a leader must begin and end all work. At the beginning, it's like looking in a crystal ball, using the data and work of the crew to figure out where we're going. And at the end, it's about looking back to see how far we've come, so we can project how much further we can go. Visionaries are also responsible for maintaining hope in the work, the mission, and the crew. You see the target, and keep your eye on that goal, even when we miss sometimes. This has to do with the last section, too, about focus.

So how do you share that vision? How do you keep everyone on task and get to the point of success in the mission and vision?

**That's what the next section is all about:** *create that STRATEGY PLAN that will drive all that you do into the future, so your business can abide and thrive.*

# THE BUSINESS

## *Your Blueprint for STRATEGY PLANNING*

Why don't more American businesses have a plan?

*Strategy Planning is hard.*

One reason it's hard is that the decisions you make in your strategy session will be with you a long time. The idea is to set a direction for the organization for the next 1-10 years, depending on your situation. The 12-18-month plan has more detail, including points of executions key performance indicators, and personnel assignments, to mention a few. The longer-term strategies, 2-10 years or so, are much more general, laying out concepts without the details. You want to know the overall mission, but the specifics will be adjusted each year to accommodate current situations, technology, staffing, and so on.

Another challenge is that it takes time to work through the plan, and you don't always see quick, tangible results after the many meetings you attend to work with the group to write the plan. So, it can get discouraging. Humans like instant gratification, which is one reason why my planning sessions include the design of a visual aid. More on that later.

The thing is, having a strategy is a critical component to building best practices and getting your organization to the next level. This is a fact easily demonstrated by a number of analogies and real-life examples. I've read that only 20% of American businesses have a strategy in place. Of those, in my personal experience, only about half actually use it and follow the plan.

According to OnStrategy,

- 95% of a typical workforce doesn't understand its organization's strategy

- 90% of organizations fail to execute their strategies successfully

- 86% of executive teams spend less than one hour per month discussing strategy

- 60% of organizations don't link strategy to budgeting

Besides the fact that I love the process, it's the main reason I wanted to write this book. Business in the U.S. is critical to our capitalist society. If more businesses would plan properly, we'd be more prosperous. That prosperity is then useful in so many ways, for the employees, stakeholders, beneficiaries of philanthropy, and more.

And like most things, it helps to prepare before you start the process. They say painting is 95% prep and clean up and only 5% actual painting. In our case, we'll spend about 15 hours prepping, five to ten hours in the actual planning session with the group, and four to six hours cleaning up and sharing the documentation including the visual aid. Implementation is a whole different story, and some helpful information is included in section three (and in the companion workbook).

Who is at risk if there is no plan? Oh, where do I even begin? How about: everyone?

Third generation owners need a plan so all of the family can agree on what has to happen when Grandad really retires. This is the time in family businesses where most fail. So be sure that the grandkids are interested, involved and engaged in the planning so they will be successful later.

Partnerships need a plan to be sure they all agree on the overall direction for the long game. One of the most important things about creating a plan, or any business documentation like job descriptions, values statements and policies, is the communication that happens around the process of writing these important documents. At the very least, it forces us to talk to each other.

Giant corporations need a plan so that they can get all the employees rowing in the same direction. We'll talk about CREW and implementation in section three, but they can't get you where you want to go if you don't give them a map.

Solopreneurs need a plan to 1. Stay small and solo, if that's the desire or 2. Grow carefully so they don't out grow their own time and fail because of too much demand. Don't spend so much time on the thing you do that you forget to work on the business itself. Work ON the business, not just IN it.

Nonprofits need a plan to be sure they are serving their clients in the most effective way, and handling everything so that they can live up to the inevitable scrutiny. I work with a lot of non-profits, having been in that world for 15 years, and I'm even certified as a non-profit manager.

It's a significant responsibility for everyone to run a business. *Having a plan helps us all to share the burden and the fun!*

**So, let's jump in. Before you can build the actual plan, it helps to ask a few questions...**

## WHO needs to be in the room with the facilitator when you actually sit down to write this strategy?

### There are several philosophies to explore:

### (1) The TOP DOWN Idea

Many firms want the high-level strategy to be driven by the C Suite. Those folks who are tasked by ownership *(whether it's private or stock)* are asked to create and execute the strategy. This is appropriate, since the folks at that level are keenly aware on a general level of the bigger picture, government regulations, ownership issues and needs, budgets, staffing environment, competition, and a vast array of other overall factors. They are, essentially, the architects. They don't build the building, though.

I am often asked if the board should be involved in the strategy planning. Usually, the answer is a qualified "No." Bringing the whole board is too much, but having representation by one or two from the board is a good idea. It's a very specific decision and every firm needs to consider this carefully. For example, non-profit firms will usually have much more board representation than for-profit firms do. Family owned businesses have to decide based on very personal criteria. Precedents are set in times like this, and so having the board member(s) who are forward thinkers that won't get caught in paralysis by analysis or try to micromanage the process *(during or afterward)* is critical. You want your board members to be champions of the strategy later, so having that mindset can make all the difference in successful execution.

### (2) The REPRESENT ALL Idea

Since the C-Suite doesn't have to be on the ground with the drills and hammers, it's often a good idea to include one or two folks to represent that element in the organization. It's usually a line manager or director, someone who deals day to day with the crew but has the ability to see the vision and think beyond next month's numbers. This person would need the support of the executives in the room and enough gumption to speak up loudly when they see a problem in the plan from the perspective of actually executing the ideas being discussed. A good facilitator will help that person be heard, and also help that person see beyond their own limitations if needed.

### (3) The UP-AND-COMERS Idea

Another group that could be represented are the up and comers. These are the folks who are the hope of the future of the firm, the ones who are seen by everyone else as high potential to stay a long time and eventually rise to management. They are not yet managers or directors, and perhaps don't have much time in with the company yet. These folks bring a perspective from their newness that is valuable because they aren't entrenched yet in that death trap of "we've always done it this way" mindset. These folks may need a little education or preparation before the meeting to understand the process and language used, especially if they aren't on the business side of the business, like accounting or HR, but the specialists, engineers, or technical types.

### WHY are we doing the plan itself?

Are we doing a new plan for the right reasons? If you don't have one, then that's reason enough.

But if you do have a plan already, why are you doing it again? Is it really old? Has something fundamental to your organization changed, such as new ownership or a change in the customer base or a regulation that caused the need to restructure your processes?

This question is important because before you start, you need a real commitment to finish, to be willing to adjust the organizational structure, to see it through to the end. For example, when you decide to make the plan, you may find you are going to need to add divisions, staff, or products. You may realize you need to rework the culture a bit. You may find you should rearrange the department, rename job titles, and more. Every strategy creates change in the organization, and if you don't have the capacity to accept that change right now, it's best to wait until you do before you try to create a new plan. Sometimes, you have to get the house in order before you do any remodeling.

### WHAT are we trying to accomplish?

If it's your first planning process ever, the needs are different if you are a brand-new business vs. an older business that just hadn't ever done any planning.

If it's a brand-new business, and you want to start out with a solid plan for success, kudos to you for thinking this way.

By mapping out the strategy now, your business will be a long-term success in the end. You'll have to make lots of assumptions, though, and much of the plan will be based on industry research and not historical data. So, the understanding of your vertical, the capital requirements you'll need, the people, processes and profit capacities may be based on some assumptions. That's OK, because you're still ahead of the game by having a plan at all.

If you're an established business that hasn't had a plan before, you'll have more data, presumably, that can be used to help understand what to do next. In this case, change is imminent, so the conversation above about your level of commitment is critical. There may be a need to increase education and the culture of long term thinking within your crew to help them see why we need to do this.

Are you just updating an old plan? You may want to review the old plan and see what still works. If you are just refreshing objectives, that is a different process than if you are missing some of the elements or modernizing. You may find that you can keep some things in place, especially if there has been demonstrated value. By refreshing and updating what works, you can build cultural continuity. But, if you haven't seen value, or if you plan is a long wordy document that no one reads and collects dust, it may be worth starting over entirely.

Are you starting a new business/division/product line? Each entity should have its own strategy, but not necessarily each product or division. And for the values section, there is a strong argument that every entity within a single ownership/holding company should be agreeable to the same values across the enterprise, because the values statements are culture building tools. Some even want the same vision statement across the enterprise. We'll get into the differences later, but it is relevant if one entity or division needs a refresher and another doesn't.

Are you hoping for the plan to reinvigorate the crew? It always does, in fact.

Assuming a thoughtful communication plan, they will respond to the new plan with a renewed energy. When leaders explain the process in advance, include the right people in the process, and share the final results appropriately, the number one response, in my experience, is a sense of security in the organization. Your crew wants to know that their leaders are taking care of the big picture and that you know what direction you're all headed.

**WHEN must we complete the various elements?**

When do you want the plan itself to be finished? What's the target date to have the visual aid done? When will we be rolling out the plan to the crew? When should the tactical decisions be made, and who should be involved in that process? The tactical plans are separate from strategy, so it's important to set deadlines for those elements to be completed.

Once you decide when you want the plan finished, it'll help you back into the time frame for starting the work.

### WHERE should we meet?

This is important! You need the right environment to encourage creativity. This really should not be done on site in your office; too many distractions are available. And, on breaks, while it's OK to check email and phones, it's not OK to run back to the office. We need a continuous stream of thought and that sort of interruption isn't helpful.

Comfort is important too. If the room is too small, too hot, too noisy, etc. it's hard to focus. We need the crew relaxed so their brains can function at peak capacity. Give them lots of space to move about, spread out their notes, and so on. Have snacks and drinks available IN the room, so that they can get up to refresh without missing any of the conversations.

You'll want a room with whiteboards, space for flip chart paper to be posted on the wall and everyone to be able to walk around and view those or even write on them during some of the exercises. *(Room layout and supplies checklists are featured in the companion workbook.)*

### HOW do we implement in such a way that we make the time we spent worth it?

Implementation plan requirements, including an accountability process, tracking, and timeline of events will help everyone stay on track. Team building exercises both before and after the actual strategy session can help enhance communication and trust.

You may need a third-party strategy coach or facilitator who will keep the group on track. At a minimum you need to assign the task of accountability leader to someone. Give it a cool name, and don't rely only on management staff. You may have someone in the ranks that is great at motivating and tracking details who can keep the plan moving even though they aren't a direct line manager.

The plan itself can take hundreds of forms, which is another challenge. I like the KISS principle *(Keep It Simple, Stupid)* so this book will center on a one-page overall plan, for the bigger picture, with several implementation systems and pages to keep you on track in the tactical process that ensures success.

There are questions to answer about your organization that will help guide you with regard to answering these who, what, when, why, how questions.

- What is the culture of your organization?

- What motivates your team to move?

- How do we keep the motivation up?

- How does the Board want the reporting done?

- Does your board accept that the plan is a long-term plan or does every board chair want a new one? This is a really big question for non-profit organizations.

- Do we have enough people to do all this and keep the real work moving? *(A tip: this IS "real work" and don't let anyone tell you otherwise.)*

There are no shortcuts. Every part of the plan must be completed to make it work. Don't worry, you'll get everything you need here *(and in the companion workbook)* to make this happen.

**Generally, you'll also see a <u>RULE OF THREE</u>:**

Three MEETINGS: *For Creating & Communicating the Plan*

Three CONCEPTS: *Broad Strategic Pillars*

Three KPIs per Pillar

Three COMMITTEES: *One per pillar*

Three YEARS: *With 1-year updates and a 10-year long view*

Three-MONTH INCREMENTS: *Quarterly measurements*

*Remember: the plan is only the beginning.* Once the plan is finished, and communicated, the entire structure of the organization needs to match.

**We'll explore the plan basics in the next few chapters, from TOP TO BOTTOM:**

- Values
- Vision
- Mission
- Strategy
- Objectives, KPIs, tactics
- Accountability

***Now, let's do this!***

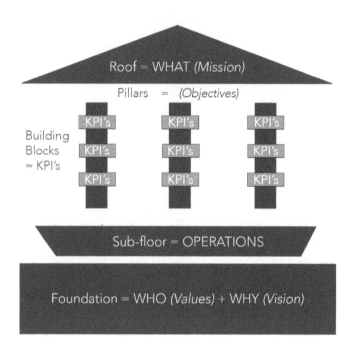

Everthing must rise from the FOUNDATION *(Values & Vision)*
and fit under the ROOF *(Mission)*.

# VALUES: *The "who are we" section*

The first piece of the foundation is the definition of WHO you are as an entity. I call this your values statement, and it's both a public message and internal guide to the big decisions. It's the short phrase or list of words that defines how you want to be seen by the outside world. It's your guide to creating the type of culture you want in your shop. And it's the code by which your employees are hired, trained, disciplined or fired. It can even help define the type of clients you want to serve. So, consider brushing off your value statement and check to see how well you've lived it, assuming you have one. Update it if needed. Get your team involved in the process.

Every organization lives by a set of values, whether they do it intentionally or not. Those values are what create, mold, build and sustain the company culture *(intentionally, or not)*. You want to build your culture with intention, knowingly, because everything about the company is then build on this foundation. Your hiring, firing, sales methods, marketing messages, stakeholder communications, vendor relationships, customers dynamics...every relationship you have will be built on this foundation of values.

That's why the book started with leadership analogies based on building a house. Strong leaders are needed to build the firm foundation of values upon which to place your cultures, your pillars of strategy, the building blocks of your plan, and your mission. This foundation is critical, and even a great company can't last long without it. Usually, a company is great because of the consistent, disciplined adherence to strong values.

So, would not it be better to create your culture intentionally, and with purpose, instead of relying on hope and instinct? "Hope is not a strategy" is a favorite quote by Vince Lombardi. I am not really a big football fan (my game is baseball) but I love that concept.

And absolutely everything you do grows out of those values. But what do we mean by values? What's the difference between all these catch phrases about values, vision, mission, etc.?

Values answer the question "who are we?" Your definition of who you will be as an organization should be evident when you put together your values list or statement.

**Using the house analogy, *your values are the cornerstone of your foundation.***

So, you would usually want lots of input about defining those *values*. This is the section that will take the longest, because it's the most important. This one should have the widest range of input, because it's the most important. And this is the one that will almost never change. This one undergirds everything else, so it has to be right the first time.

Think about the common clichés, and avoid them: We are the best. We have high integrity. We love our customers. We provide value. These are all much too generic.

We want to build very specific concepts into your values list or statement: How are you demonstrating integrity? How do you provide value? Where is your heart on these things? Values are generally heart centered, and often instinctual.

So, think about your daily interactions with your crew or customers. What are the values you want to see demonstrated by them every day? Who are your best people? Who are your best customers? What makes them the best? Why do you enjoy the interactions?

**Make a long list of the values words that resonate with you. You may come up with 50 to 60 words! Every word could finish one of these statements:**

We are ___.

We share ____.

We feel _____.

We are honest. We are loving. We are loyal. We are caring. We are passionate. We are careful. We are safe. We are valuable. We are daring. We are enlightened. We are diverse....empowering, reliable, consistent, servants, systematic, viable, educational, neighborly, inspiring, resourceful, dedicated, desirable, teachable, brave, nurturing, invested, persevering, adventurous, energizing, positive, consistent, forgiving, focused, pleasant, assertive, trusting, aligned, sustaining, emotional, pioneers, experts, scholarly, optimistic, forgiving, influencing, patient, present, empathetic, thorough, thoughtful, technical, astute, fun, disciplined, open, nourishing, visionary, innovative, disruptive, technical, trusted, aspiring, resourceful, credible, respect, responsive, smart, adventurous, bold, active, confident, convicted, humble, methodical, grateful, seeking, thriving, curious, developing, accountable!

We share encouragement.

We feel thoughtful.

*You get the idea!*

All of these seem like positive, healthy statements for you to use to describe your ideal employee, client, vendor, stakeholder. But they don't all apply to you. Adventurous and careful might not mesh well. You may be highly technical and thoughtful but that may mean you aren't as nimble, for example. You'll need to come up with several dozen words that actually describe who you are as a company, and then, the hard part is next.

I have seen the best success with <u>no more</u> than six (6) of these words to use in your values statement. And all of the companies under your ownership/holding company should align with these values. So, it's going to take a little time to select the right six words to describe WHO YOU ARE.

The more words you get in the first pass, the better. All of the words collected should be used in the marketing and messaging all throughout. The full list is highly valuable to continue to describe your culture well past the implementation of the strategy plan, so don't lose the longer list. We're culling the values statement itself to six of the words, but that doesn't mean we can't use all the descriptors in other areas!

**Now, the decision needs to be made about how to phrase the statement. There are several options:**

## Make a LIST

You may just select four to six words that you have in a list, and leave it at that.

## Make an ALLITERATION

Or, you can find a way to make them an alliteration, such as:

*Servants, Stewards, Spiritual, Steadfast, Sharing.*
*Timely, Trusting, Technical, Team, Thankful, Tolerant.*

## Make an ACRONYM

Or you can make an acronym, etc., essentially using the letters to make a seventh word that fits. One client had a list that spelled "GIPSIS" which was a take on a word used often in his industry. Another was able to spell out HELPER. This doesn't always work, but when it does it's useful.

You can be creative! Remember, the idea is that it's so short and easy to remember that you can count on your crew to be able to rattle off the vales any time. If it's too long, they won't remember, and neither will your clients.

## Make a SENTENCE

You could create a short sentence with the six words, as long as it doesn't dilute the memorable nature of the phrase.

## Make a RHYME

Sometimes, we can find a way to make a rhyme or rhythm to the phrase, to increase the memory.

Be careful that you aren't getting into marketing phrases or jingles too much. It's serious business, and it will certainly inform your marketing but be resolute about this being a real descriptor for your culture, and a guide for your actions.

## How will you use Values?

**HIRING**: when interviewing, as how the person has demonstrated a few of the values with a story about something real that happened. Do this before you share what the list of values are. They will be on the website, so if the person has done their homework, they will know them *(and presumably, liked them enough to consider working there).*

**TRAINING**: during orientation and training, review the values and describe what they mean. Give examples.

**FIRING**: every review should have an element of measuring if the employee has been demonstrating the values *(or not).* Find a way to do this and talk about it frequently.

**TEAM BUILDING**: how are you using the values to bring people together? Are you having games & contests that help them remember and use the values? Do you reward them based on hearing stories of how they shared the values by how they helped a client?

**CUSTOMER SELECTION**: you don't have to sell to everyone. If you find you have clients that aren't profitable, check their values. You may have a poor fit between your company and theirs.

# VISION: *the "why we do this" section*

The second layer of the foundation of your culture is your *Vision Statement.*

If you have read Simon Sinek's book *Start with Why*, you have a lot of this in mind already. Simon laid the groundwork for these discussions, and I have great respect for his positive impact on the business community. His work is inspiring and timely.

For our purposes in building a *Strategy Plan*, the conversation about WHY is only slightly different.

*So, why are you in this business?*

This is not about your budget, or your revenue projections. We can do lots of things to make money. Why did we pick this thing? One way to ponder this is to consider what your impact will be on your world. You may be doing something that has a very large impact on a smaller community, or a small impact on the entire planet, or both. The point of vision is to see how you'll affect the future, the big picture, in the long run. This is a no holds barred exercise, looking out 5, 10 or 100 years. What will be the legacy you leave? You might think of *Vision* as your *purpose statement*, if that helps.

> CAUTION: This is a philosophical statement, helping others understand the reason why you're taking on your mission, but vision is not mission. This is not your statement to describe what you do; that's your mission statement and it comes next. This is the statement sharing the results of your mission, the impact you'll have, the changes you'll create, the improvement on lives of others that you seek.

There are many occasions where someone in one of my Foundational Strategy Workshops will misunderstand this question: Why are we in business? They will answer "to make money." That's a non-starter. That is not a vision statement. Making money is a given; if you don't make money you go out of business. If you were only there to make money, why not rob banks? The questions are more about why you do this particular thing, why you've chosen recycling or chemical manufacturing or workforce development to make your living versus the many thousands of other options.

So, share with us your vision, your why, your impact that you hope to make on the world. Help us in your strategy statements to show us why the world will be better because of your business.

Is your vision to help young women into leadership? Is your vision to help feed the world? Is your vision to bring justice to those who are underrepresented? Is your vision to provide mobility to people who have had limbs damaged? What is the vision of your company for the world that you live in? Sometimes you just find it makes a difference in your own neighborhood and that's wonderful. Sometimes you are trying to make a difference globally.

As I write this book we have been in isolation because of the corona virus. The whole world will remember COVID-19 and the problems that were caused. Many businesses have added and/or changed their direction so they could help.

When your vision is to feed the world and distribution becomes a problem due to a pandemic, you could pivot and use a distribution chain to get food to people. When the vision for your company is to create chemicals that grow food better, faster and more nutritiously but you have the equipment to make hand sanitizer, you make hand sanitizer and cleaning agents so that the pandemic can be slowed. These are unprecedented times and for a little while everyone's vision of changing the world and meditating the virus has coalesced. It's a crazy emotional time, where strategies and strategic planning and key performance indicators have sort of gone out the window. But as we began to slowly reopen the world, we are realizing that things will go back to normal and while there may be small adjustments to our strategies, business will eventually get back to normal. Staying the course, sticking to your map, getting your business back on track and keeping it on track when we all have crises *(pandemics or something else...)* can only be accomplished when you have the documentation you need to build the plans and structure and to make things work again. The vision helps your business abide after the crisis.

## MISSION: *the "what" it is that you do section*

This is quite familiar to most businesses organizations. Many already have a document, plaque or web page dedicated to the mission. It's an externally used statement, telling the world what you want to contribute. Internally, it helps your crew understand the "big rocks" of their day to day activities. Who will be your customers? What geographic markets will you serve? Will you be creating a product, a service, or both? This is an action statement. This statement is short, direct, and will fit on the back of your business cards. If your organization is large enough, you may need to have a *mission statement* for each division. *This is your WHAT — what do we do, as an entity, to meet our long-term vision?*

What you're doing, your action, your mission equals the answer to that question what is our product or service. You cannot and should not answer this question until you have fully embraced values and vision. Even if you already have the products lined up and your services developed, you want to define that only after you build the foundation of values and vision.

> The mission is the umbrella, or roof, of your business. Everything you do should grow out of the vision and values of the foundation of your business and fit under the roof of your mission.

We get off track on mission a lot. Most of us, with the best of intentions, experience what the IT world calls "scope creep." We get distracted and we chase after the latest new shiny thing. If that is happening to you, get your map back out! Look again at the architecture of your business to keep you on track.

*Mission* is just what you do in order to accomplish the *vision* of your business. That mission statement can definitely use some of the words that you developed in your values mapping process — make use of a few of the words that weren't selected for the vision. It's good to use those words to build a statement. As with values and vision, a one sentence mission statement is adequate! You don't have to explain it all in that sentence; just say enough so people can understand.

Long-range strategy objectives come next. This is simply the process of looking down the road 3 to 5 years to determine where you will be organizationally and how you will get there. You should consider everything, from client base to employees needed to the financial impact of each decision. This is not a step to take lightly. Without it, you simply career into the future without direction. Even if your business is booming and you are rolling in money, you may be a runaway train heading for the washed-out bridge. The last surviving buggy whip manufacturer was probably happy about the monopoly, but in the end if they didn't pivot they died.

One common excuse for failing to conduct long-range planning is lack of time. You have as much time as anyone else, and if you don't make it a priority, the consequences are significant. Sure, you may still get rich, but you might have been richer, or made a bigger impact, or helped more people. So, take the time to look down the tracks and decide what you want the organization to look like in 5 years. Dream big, and adjust as you go.

## THE REST *is the HOW*

So now we know who we are, why we're doing it and what we want to do. The next step is to figure out HOW we're going to do it. *How we hold that roof of mission up over the foundation of vision and values?* This, finally, completes STRATEGY. This strategy, your plan, your action, comes from what I like to call the *pillars of your business (the objectives) and KPI's.* Some books call this the big rocks. The pillars of your business encompass 3 to 4 major sections or verticals that you have to manage in order to be successful. These pillars are different for every business.

What is the same for every business is that all of us probably need a pillar or strategy called people. All of us have a strategy around finances. Perhaps we all need a strategy around product or service or customers. What I have learned is that during these workshops is that people decide to frame the pillars a certain way based on values.

So, for example on the financial pillar, some have called it the stewardship pillar. Some call it a fiscal responsibility. Some just say money! That's OK too. But the point is they are describing their financial pillar in a way that fits the culture and language of the organization. Words matter.

One of the descriptors could be pulled from your list of VALUE words from earlier. Everyone needs to have a financial pillar. Yet, I never allowed the actual dollars to be used anywhere on the one page, poster size, visual aid that we create at the end of the workshop. There's a reason for this. You remember we talked about how we are not in this for the money? Instead, we are in this to do a certain type of job that leaves a legacy that honors our values, and that activity will lead to the money. So, if your fiscal strategy just puts in a dollar amount, there will be issues: you may not want that information public. If the fiscal pillar has growth of 10% in the customer base, that's acceptable. A fiscal pillar might say "increase net revenue by a percentage." A fiscal pillar might say "add 100 clients to our business." Those are fine but we try to avoid dollar values because we want this to be a public document.

Also, it doesn't support a healthy culture internally if all you care about is the money. It really helps when we can put our one page visual aid on the website and in packets to new employees, etc. so that everyone really understands not only that we have a map *(which only 20% of companies do)* but also that we care about it enough to publish it. It is transparent to the world.

Customers like to see that you are planning this way, too. It gives them confidence in your abilities. Each pillar helps you then define those major strategies that will keep your business moving. For illustration purposes, let's say you have a fiscal pillar, a people pillar, and then you need one more and you want it to be called an innovation pillar. Let's make sure that innovation is one of your values, first. Or maybe your third pillar has to do with something very specific in the near term. One client of mine had their third pillar for certain fiscal year to build a new building. Clearly, they are not going to build a new building every year. But, over the next 18 months it was a critical component of continuing to thrive in your business, so we used it.

Sometimes I find a company that really needs four objective pillars. Usually we try to stop at four, otherwise it gets too cumbersome. Four big rocks/pillars/strategies in any given 18-month period is enough.

Once you have those, you'll find you need the KPIs — key performance indicators — or what I call the building blocks on each pillar. The fiscal pillar might have three or four building blocks such as:

- increase number of customers by 10%

- increase prospecting database by 50%

- reduce expenses by 5%

- find a new Accounting System

Your people pillar might have elements that are about your own crew and elements about your customers. Or you may choose to separate the employee vs. customer pillars. It depends on the priority for the next few months. If you have a separate customer pillar from your employee/crew pillar you may have only three items on each.

The number of items is important. Consider this: if you have three strategic pillars and each pillar has three items that's nine items. One of my mentors calls this the three by three. That means that you have nine things to focus on during the year in only 12 months. That's plenty.

No one is suggesting that you can actually get everything done from a simple one-page visual aid concept. The tactical decisions that are going to help you achieve each of those building blocks/KPIs will have several pages of tactical planning! Which we will discuss next. But the STRATEGY will all fit on the one page, to give everyone an overview as to what direction we are going. Implementation will be critical.

Having each pillar contain three KPIs *(and each KPI has a couple of pages of tactical plans. \*See companion workbook)* is manageable, measurable, reasonable, and achievable. And, your crew will have that visual aid all around them, as will other stakeholders, which guides implementation.

**Everything we do must rise from the FOUNDATION of our *Values* and *Vision* and fit under the ROOF of our *Mission*.**

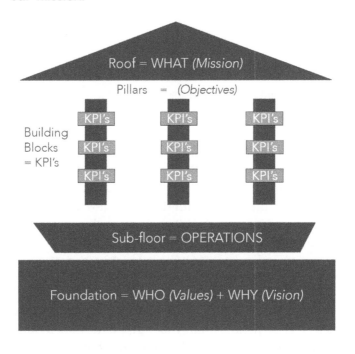

# SAMPLE *Strategy Plans*

**Our Mission: Build Better Bosses**

| Author & Keynote | Strategy Workshops | Executive Coach |
|---|---|---|
| Better Communication. Better Crew. | Better Plan. Better Profit. | Better Decisions. Better Destiny. |
| Clarifying Your Future. | Helping Business Abide. | Keeping Leaders Focused. |
| Communication Training (6) | Corporate Clients (12) | Vistage CEOs (16) |
| Books & Blogs (1/24) | Pro-bono/Non-profits (4) | Other Vistage (22) |
| Platform Keynote (3) | Build Licensing Plan | Private Clients (12) |

**Operations: Diane and Wendy**

**Our Values: Truth, Friendship, Service, Grace**

**Our Vision: Joy in the Workplace**

ABIDING STRATEGY 2022-2025
*[Printed with permission.]*

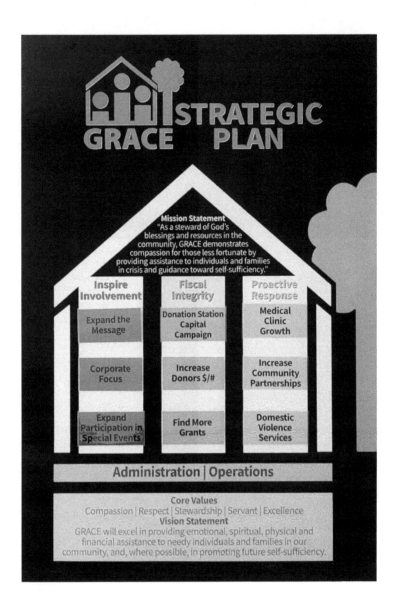

GRACE STRATEGIC PLAN

**Mission Statement**
"As a steward of God's blessings and resources in the community, GRACE demonstrates compassion for those less fortunate by providing assistance to individuals and families in crisis and guidance toward self-sufficiency."

| Inspire Involvement | Fiscal Integrity | Proactive Response |
|---|---|---|
| Expand the Message | Donation Station Capital Campaign | Medical Clinic Growth |
| Corporate Focus | Increase Donors $/# | Increase Community Partnerships |
| Expand Participation in Special Events | Find More Grants | Domestic Violence Services |

**Administration | Operations**

**Core Values**
Compassion | Respect | Stewardship | Servant | Excellence
**Vision Statement**
GRACE will excel in providing emotional, spiritual, physical and financial assistance to needy individuals and families in our community, and, where possible, in promoting future self-sufficiency.

(GRACE) *Grapevine Relief and Community Exchange*
*[Printed with permission.]*

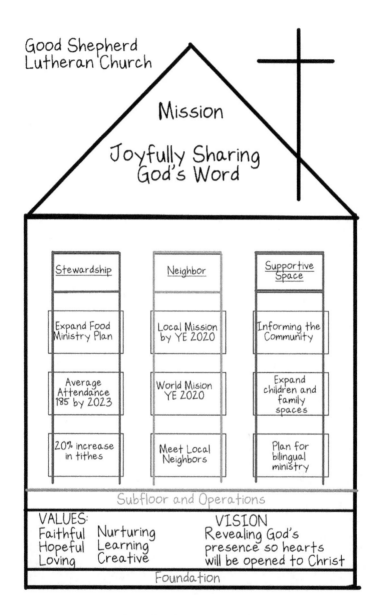

Good Shepherd Lutheran Church

Mission

Joyfully Sharing God's Word

Stewardship

Expand Food Ministry Plan

Average Attendance 185 by 2023

20% increase in tithes

Neighbor

Local Mission by YE 2020

World Mision YE 2020

Meet Local Neighbors

Supportive Space

Informing the Community

Expand children and family spaces

Plan for bilingual ministry

Subfloor and Operations

VALUES:
Faithful   Nurturing
Hopeful   Learning
Loving    Creative

VISION
Revealing God's presence so hearts will be opened to Christ

Foundation

Good Shepherd Lutheran Church
*[Printed with permission.]*

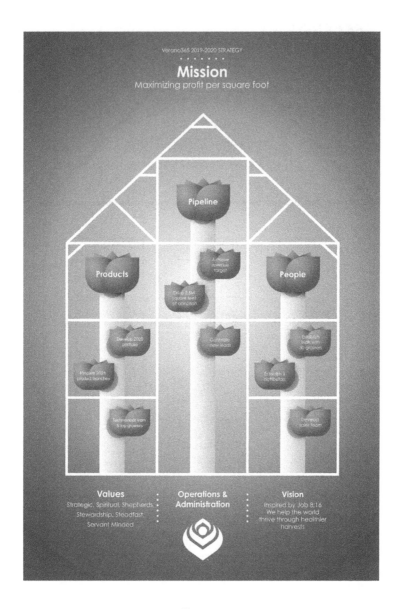

Verano
*[Printed with permission.]*

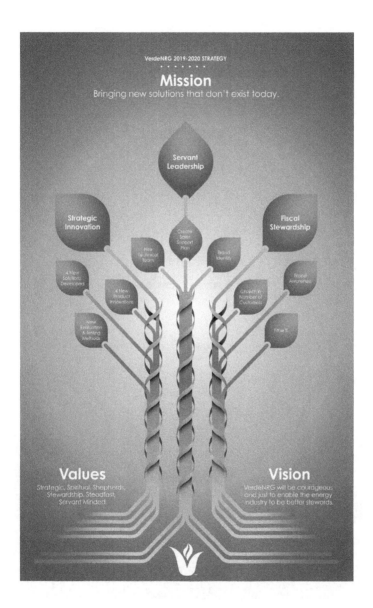

Verde NRG
*[Printed with permission.]*

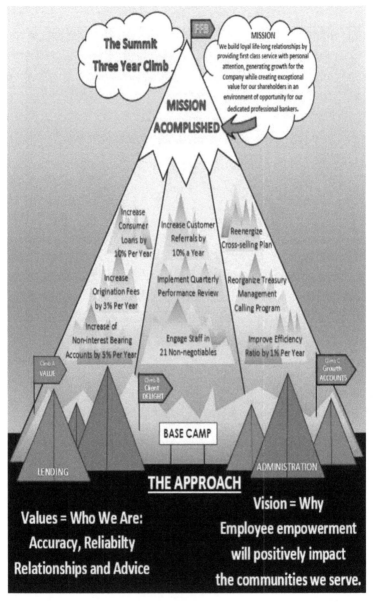

FFIN
[Printed with permission.]

# THE CREW

## *Your BEST TEAM to Deliver THE VISION*

Now that we have figured out how to be leaders who BUILD, and we have a methodology for creating a long-lasting plan that helps clarify intention and align goals, how do we engage the crew and actually get things done?

*First...Why CREW and not TEAM?*

It's personal privilege as the author, but I don't care for the use of the word team when referring to your staff. There are a few reasons for that, and it may be helpful for you, too.

A team is a great thing! Having a team spirit, learning to win together, having the comradery of a team mascot and so on inspires everyone. It's not that there is anything wrong with the word.

CREW, first of all, is simply a different word to use with essentially the same meaning. Solely for the reason that it is different, we think differently about the concept. We could say troop or herd or squad or staff or company or congress, and it would be something different to engage our brains in a new way! Because I often use the analogy that a leader must think of keeping "the ship afloat" — the business alive — above all other considerations, the word crew fits for me. And, to further the boat analogy, think of a crew rowing a boat. If they are all rowing the same direction, we have progress. If not, we have chaos. So, it is also relevant because it is incumbent upon the leader to be sure the crew knows WHAT DIRECTION to row! Hence, the Strategy Sessions! The strategy is the way the leader keeps the crew all rowing in the same, correct, direction.

There are a couple of fun *acronyms* I've used for **CREW** as well.

## Candor Raises Everyone's Wealth

Because caring candor is a hallmark of leadership, and so critical to the success of every organization, it helps to remember that the more we practice candor, the better off everyone will be.  We don't have to be mean and we can practice kindness. We can show our crew, and each other, the facts of any situation even when it's uncomfortable and we need to apply some correction.

## Clarify, Reward, Engage, Win

I find this one to be even more helpful. As leaders, what steps can we take to be sure our message is heard? How can we motivate everyone involved to do their best, align with the company and each other, and bring us to the next level of excellence, no matter where we've started? The four basic steps can be shown in the four words *Clarify, Reward, Engage, Win.*

## Clarify

Without clarity in our mission, vision and values, the crew doesn't know how their actions impact the long-term health of the company. If they don't know the plan, or have a map, how can they get us down the road to a brilliantly accomplished mission? We can provide all the forms and processes to report back to management the activities of the week. If the activities don't align, though, because leaders aren't clear about the RESULTS they need from the crew, a lot of time will be wasted.

That's why the day-to-day tactical planning has to clearly line up with the *Values*, *Vision*, *Mission* and *Strategies*. The objectives must be public and often repeated. Only then can the tactics bring us where we need to go. This is the most misunderstood element of strategy planning. Most stop too soon, and the silver thread of activity that should *connect the plan with the process* is never implemented.

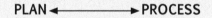

PLAN ◄──────────► PROCESS

## Reward

For human beings to stay motivated, there must be some kind of reward. We can endure the worst suffering, if we know the reward is coming at the end — whether that reward is just survival or if it's the accomplishment of a lifelong dream. And the level of reward should always match the effort, of course. One of our greatest challenges as leaders is figuring out what rewards to use. If we are too generous, we don't match the effort needed to profit and grow the company. If too stingy, we have the same effect. Motivation comes when we give enough reward to leave the crew wanting more, without them feeling the effort isn't worth it. This seems obvious, but in my experience, the desire to make all things even, and the same, company-wide, jinxes the result. Rewards can match up to the staff person, too! Allowing some flexibility and choice will help everyone find what works for their own inspiration. Add that to the clarity of the mission, values and vision, helping folks realize the impact they will have on the world, and you have a good recipe for success.

## Engage

Engagement is now a well understood corporate need. The Gallup studies outlined in *First, Break All the Rules* are legendary in strong corporations now. The Q12 surveys for engagement have been proven time and again to help companies grow stronger and more profitable with more joy and lower turnover. The difference between employee satisfaction and employee engagement are well documented! We don't need to repeat those wonderful lessons here, but if you haven't read Buckingham's work, et al, I highly recommend it.

## Win

Winning is in our nature! All humans have the need for survival, and that looks a lot like winning in our culture. We have thousands of measures by which we track our winnings – love, money, jewelry, children, houses, cars, toys, clothing, health and much more. When we clarify, reward and engage our crew, we all can win in whatever way motivates us to get up and do it again every day.

## *Go Get A CREW*

Once you've figured out how you're going to handle being a leader for your crew, you have to go get a crew! Sometimes, we have to move folks around as we shift our strategies, objectives and tactics. Sometimes, we are a new business and realize we can't go it alone. More often, we find we've grown to a point that takes us to that critical junction of hiring just in time to manage the growth without wrecking the bottom line. Whatever situation you're in, there are some golden nuggets here for you regarding the life-cycle of employment.

Have you noticed how the "jobless" rate has been bouncing around a lot lately? Up one week, down the next, so that we might even be lulled into a sense of complacency — or confusion. Are there employees out there, or not? Are they any good? Why are they available? How do I know which ones are the good ones to hire?

It would be nice if we could just keep all the good employees we already have, and if no one would retire, move to the firm across the street, or leave for any reason! In addition to hiring well, you can actually help reduce your own turnover with some of what we discuss today — and avoid having to go through this so often. One website, the HRcapitalist.com, cites turnover rates for service industries at 20-25%. But in the hospitality industry, for example, it's been cited at 37-100%! For telemarketing, it's even worse.

You have probably interviewed dozens of candidates over the years, and for some of us it's much easier than others. Here's a quick checklist of ideas for handling hiring; you have to LISTEN. No, really, you have to listen carefully, all the time, to the needs of your crew. We'll talk about that later. But it's also another acronym *(see a pattern here?)* too, for the basic steps of building a great crew.

### Locate

We have so many more options now — newspapers, trade magazines, on-line services, recruiters, Facebook, other social media, hobby clubs, etc. The trouble is that if you just send out dozens of messages on all these sources, it's like shotgun sales — you're sending the word out to anyone who can read, but the job probably has very specific skill sets required *(no matter which position it is)*. Remember the old life insurance prospecting joke? "Who's a prospect?" "Anyone who can fog a mirror!"

So, perhaps you could try target marketing for new employees the way you do for clients. Of course, you'll want to prepare well. This is the time to review what the job duties are and to be sure the job descriptions are up to date. Then, look in some new and original places. For great customers service reps, look at places where you have experienced great customer service. I once hired someone from a pizza joint. She was a great waitress. A few from our office were regulars at lunch, and she always remembered us. She turned out to be a terrific Customer Service Rep. Or maybe you can hire from within one of your target industries. If you sell insurance to golf courses, you might talk to the vendor's representative that sells them their golf carts or fertilizer. That person in the parallel field knows the industry, has connections, and just might be ready for a change.

And if you are going to advertise, go beyond the newspaper *(even if it's online)*. Place an ad in the appropriate trade magazines. If someone finds out about the position you have available because they are avid readers of one of the many great industry specific publications, perhaps from your own trade association, then you know you have someone who is serious about a career in your industry.

Some have had success at the colleges: career days, alumni groups, business clubs, and the like.

Employee referral programs work very well too. What a great measure of how well you're treating your current crew. If the folks who work for you are getting their friends and family to line up for a job there, you're doing a lot of things right!

### Interview

Please be prepared. Having a list of questions that you'll ask each person is a great idea — consistency in the questions means you'll have a good basis of comparison when all the interviews start to run together in your head! Many of the profile services provide questions, such as Predictive Index, Omnia, Caliper, ZeroRisk® to name just a few. Setting up a phone interview first will give you a nice picture of their abilities with clients on the phone, if that is relevant. And you'll get to hear their enthusiasm without taking as much of your time or theirs.

Screen well, and don't be fooled by a great resume. These days, many are written by a service, and don't show you much about the writing talents of the candidate. Look for great cover letters. When candidates are answering an ad on-line, there is usually an opportunity for them to put on a cover note. How well are they doing there? Did they bother? Is proper grammar used, even though it's an on-line form? For many positions, a test of skills is in order too. Do they really know the system(s) they claim to know?

It's not a bad idea to have more than one person interview the candidate; having others take a look gives a fresh perspective. One final warning about interviews: Watch out for inappropriate questions. If the question isn't directly related to the actual work to be done, just don't ask. Small employers are not exempt from this rule. Your HR professional can help you here.

### Select

Hire to your culture! You want the candidate to be a great fit with your other staff. This is another nod to *First, Break All the Rules!* It's a great read and explains why that fit, and having a friend or two at work, can positively impact productivity. The one caution: don't hire a bunch of people that are all "like each other" when it comes to their skills and talents. Stagnation kills, and you need a diversity of personality types and talent pool to make the best team. And, you have clients of all different types. Don't be afraid to hire someone without industry experience. You have access to amazing training resources. After 15 years in the trade association space, I can assure you that every industry has a good group of peers who are in the business of keeping that industry alive and successful.

When you are very sure you have the right person, make an offer they can't refuse with benefits, perks, & extra pay for extra efforts like obtaining designations, etc. This is back to the reward element in the word crew, right?

### Train

Training starts with orientation to your firm. Take the time to give the new employee introductions all around, the grand tour, and a little history of the place. Let each department manager spend 15 minutes explaining how their group fits into the whole. Review mission statements and the like.

Make an education plan, early in that first couple of weeks, to round out whatever the new employee needs to function well. Include professional skills in addition to the requisite continuing education and professional classes. There are many wonderful sources. And hopefully you can let a senior staff person walk them through the steps of your firm's best practices!

## Engage

If you won't work to keep an employee, why bother hiring them? Turnover costs are just too high to ignore! The American Management Association estimate a few years ago stated that turnover costs equal an average of 30% of salary! There are websites that provide free "turnover calculators." Try not to figure out your specific costs! If you help employees care about the company and its mission, because you are committed to the industry and the community, you have a better chance of reducing turnover. Engage them in the growth of the business, and ask their opinions frequently. The younger generation is always sensitive to making a difference and to being heard. They want to make a contribution! Make use of all that fresh energy and let them create a plan to position your firm as a community leader.

## Nurture

I don't mean baby them! But there should be a plan of growth for each employee and it should be shared. What do you see as this employee's future? Please share it with them. Monitor progress and maintain their personal growth plan. Even if you are a small firm, and there aren't promotions to pass around, little increases in responsibilities within the same job title can make a big difference.

These steps may just help you find and keep some of the best employees out there. If you are going to the expense of hiring, you may as well listen well, and hire well!

### *Once you have the right CREW hired — you can get to IMPLEMENTATION*

<u>Apply their strengths</u>: These great folks will help you get the tactical work done on the plan. (*The Abiding Strategies Workbook* is also available to help guide you all in setting up the tactical steps, and reporting out so that everyone is in the loop.) Keeping the folks engaged is a critical element. Because you chose well at the beginning, including everyone who really should be there, you will have great buy-in for the goals and process.

<u>Setting the work groups</u>: It's important that the work groups are arranged in a way that makes sense. Can you realign department names and job titles around the Vision wording, or values, or the Strategic pillar names? Everyone, every day, will be doing something that advances the Plan. That's how we are assured the plan will abide.

<u>You can create these groups in two ways</u>:

- Assign to appropriate department, and allow it to become a part of their day to day.

- Create work groups or committees that are cross departmental

In any case, you'll want a crew chief, and it will help to have variety in the personalities and skill sets within the group. While there is a strategic leader assigned to the plan, the day to day also needs a local, hands on crew member that can help keep the process moving while working through the normal day to day short term stuff; we still have to take care of our customers' needs as they arise, etc.

These crew groups will work better in odd numbers. There needs to be a tie breaker available when they hit a snag of disagreement on a finer point of how to do something. If they are deadlocked, they have to raise it up the ladder and we don't want that. We want them to be accountable to themselves and solve as much of the tactical concerns as they can on their own.

Creating a culture of independence is much easier, and manageable, when they have the map of the Strategy Plan to guide them. And, when they do have to bring a question up to the next level, they should know that the expectation is to bring the problem and three solutions. They can't drop the problem on your shoulders as the boss! Reference the Harvard Business Review article *Who's got the Monkey* for more on this. It's a timeless lesson in delegation and authority.

*The next chapter may help your crew understand the nature of __accountability and their role in making the plan work__.*

## *Build a Foundation of Accountability within The Crew*

- Belief in the values is parallel

- Understanding the vision is illuminated

- Involvement in mission is ingrained

- Listening sustains the strategy

- Delivering results brings incentives

Accountability starts at the top, both via the understanding by all employees about why the organization takes a certain direction or process, and in having accountability modeled by the leadership of the organization. If the FOUNDATION of accountability is missing, *the MISSION and VISION won't be sustainable.*

Great leaders line up the needs of their organization with the needs of the employees, spell out the expectations of the team and create systems and rewards that ensure the best results.

***Leaders who model accountability will maximize productivity so your organization can flourish and thrive.***

## *Beliefs are Parallel — Values are Clear*

Working in parallel is harder than it sounds. Think about what parallel means: you run along at the same spot in a plane, matching velocity and keeping a certain distance. Part of the Wikipedia definition says: "parallel lines must be located in the same plane, and parallel planes must be located in the same three-dimensional space. A parallel combination of a line and a plane may be located in the same three-dimensional space."

In our example, we certainly don't mean to be that precise. The lines may even cross sometimes, but the concept is real.

Working in parallel with all the various stakeholders in our organization is tricky. We have to make the customers happy. We need the employees to be happy and productive. We have a board of directors, or an advisory group that needs to feel in sync. And we may have investors that are particularly interested in what we are doing day to day that will affect their decisions about us.

With all those folks to satisfy, how do we get started actually getting the work done, while ensuring that we are doing the right work?

Everyone needs a strong BELIEF in the values, vision, mission and strategy. If this isn't the case, the competing priorities will be a distraction at the least, and create real conflict at the worst. The strategy planning process helps align the priorities.

## FOR CONSIDERATION:

What are you doing to communicate the values of the organization with your staff to ensure parallel beliefs?

## *Understanding is Illuminated – What Results are Required?*

Be very clear about what you want, and the results that will be expected. *ILLUMINATE* and align your requirements! Once you have the big picture defined, smaller steps are decided. Break down the goals into measurable action items; being very specific about what needs to happen, when it is expected, the resources that are available *(and the limits you must place on those resources)* and how often you want updates. A note about resources: include monetary budgets, time and personnel resources. Sometimes we forget that it's not just the dollars that have to be budgeted. We are all limited on time, and sometimes the talent to do the work isn't in the building so we have to find it by way of contracting or hiring the right people.

The critical link between illumination and incentives comes in reporting. How can you be accountable for something if you aren't measuring it and then telling someone how you have done? Isn't that what accountability means? Again, per Wiki: "accountability is the acknowledgment and assumption of responsibility for actions" Or, said another way, you get to take credit! And, you can insist that your charges take credit for their actions and receive the appropriate accolades or, if they fall short, they can learn about the adjustments they need to make in their behavior.

Process is so important in all of this, especially when it comes to learning how the process can make or break you when it comes to achieving the results. Measurements and accountability with regard to the various steps taken, can give you an analysis of what works, and what doesn't. But tracking all the activities takes time and effort that many won't invest. I recommend you at least try it.

## FOR CONSIDERATION:

How are you illuminating and aligning the responsibilities of your crew to ensure proper results?

## *Involvement is Ingrained*

It helps to *involve* enough of the right people in the building out of accountability options. This is different than employee engagement, which is also important.

We're talking about how to measure results and hold everyone accountable for their actions. Can you engage and involve them in building these reports? Try to have representation from all areas of the organization in the meetings. You can't include every employee, of course; that would be unwieldy. Create a small enough group to manage the process or you may never come to a conclusion in the study. Could you bring at least one line person from each department or area of responsibility? For example: one from sales, one from accounting, one from customer service, in addition to the owners or senior staff. If possible, don't limit the meetings to managers. You have responsible employees in every area, I suspect, who are your front line and have a perspective that will be very valuable.

In fact, when you move into the tactical areas of your strategy, those line folks will help keep your expectations reasonable. You want to aim high, but not to the point of breaking. They can help you understand the resources needed to accomplish the goals you set, and the managers and owners can be sure you're not settling for too little too late. Your line folks will keep you honest, and your owners will be sure you stretch.

By ingraining a culture of inclusion and involvement, engagement increases and results go up exponentially. You build trust and create buy-in. It's well documented that the more involved someone is in setting the goals, the more excited and engaged that they will be about execution and supporting the concepts.

## FOR CONSIDERATION:

How are you creating a culture of involvement and inclusion when it comes to measuring results?

## *Listening Sustains Strategy*

No matter how well you define the mission, vision, strategies and goals, and even if you hit every target, finding a way to keep doing all those good things over time will enhance the momentum year over year. Maintaining productivity is easier if you have low employee turnover and high customer retention.

For both areas, listening to the input of others is KEY. Listening is a learned skill. If you haven't studied the art of listening, do it now. It's not the same as hearing!

Starting at the beginning always helps. Using the Abiding Strategy method creates alignment of the needs of the business, with the talents of the employees. Ask them how it fits within their world.

Further, it's a great idea to line up the tactical work that will be done against the talents of the staff doing that work. In the Gallup poll study discussed in *First, Break All the Rules* (Buckingham et al) and *Strengths Finders*, we discovered that talent is king. People that are permitted to work in areas that line up to their best talents, for at least part of everyday, are incredibly more productive. It's possible that part of this result is because they are just happier, since they are doing something that comes naturally. Success breeds success; the better they are at something, the more they will want to do it.

You may decide to take this idea to the maximum, and actually assess talents first *(see The Talent Code or Now, Discover Your Strengths)* and then re-work all the job descriptions so that everyone is doing things that fit their talents.

We often do customer satisfaction surveys. What is not often done is actual change based on those results. Nothing is more insulting. Don't ask if you really don't care.

## FOR CONSIDERATION:

What are you doing to improve your own listening skills? How well do you know your crew?

## *Delivering Results Brings Incentives*

You've created understanding about the results needed, and aligned the activities of your crew to these results.

Be sure you are providing the right <u>incentives</u>! Rewards matter. It will come as no surprise to most of you that people will respond best when properly, positively motivated. The carrot has always worked better than the stick, at least in the long run. There are great examples of how to reward folks so that they are doing the right things for you. **What gets measured gets done, but what gets rewarded gets done right.**

Don't assume they want what you want, or that the things that motivate you will motivate them. Rewards are personal.

To learn what incentives will get your employees motivated, I can only give you one piece of advice: Just ask them! A friend of mine once said "When people talk, good things happen." I believe it.

## FOR CONSIDERATION:

Do you know how your employees truly want to be rewarded?

## Reminder: Long term plans mean we have to focus on Staying the Course

You already have the up-to-date mission statement. Can you create language around that mission that empowers your internal code? Standardize everything to the values, vision and mission you developed. Don't just brand your product; brand your mission. Virtually everything you do — internal documents, external news items, meeting agendas — can be organized or communicated around those concepts. This helps the ability to focus come very naturally, no longer requiring staff to listen to pontifications about the methodology; it also helps create a habit. Even accountability is enhanced because everyone will know what direction they are going all the time.

### Now, you can celebrate!

You have all the elements of the plan, you're a better leader, and your crew knows how to get the plan into the working day to day process! Once the plan is on the wall, remember to reviewing it at least quarterly with everyone. Mark off the items completed, celebrate the wins, and keep adding to the "pillars" so that as you pull one off, you add something that didn't' make the first version.

The plan is never "DONE." Culturally the understanding that we are always looking out a few years helps the whole company stay focused on thriving, not just surviving.

**Download the FREE Companion Workbook at: AbidingStrategy.com — This will guide you through the forms and steps to create your very own plan!**

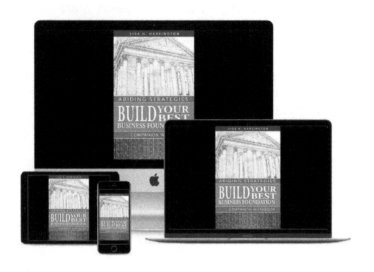

ABIDING STRATEGIES: Build Your Best Business Foundation

*FREE PDF download available at:*
**AbidingStrategy.com**

*Would you like to become CERTIFIED in the*
*Abiding Strategy® Method?*

Please email: <u>Lisa@AbidingStrategy.com</u>

# BONUS CONTENT

# — Love As Leadership —

*April 2009 - August 2020*

It wasn't the first time I'd adopted a dog just from a picture on Facebook. Surely, it won't be the last.

Maggie Mae's time with us was all too brief. When I saw the urgent post, about an elderly dachshund with bright blue eyes that was desperately trying to get out of the cage in the shelter, to the point of injuring herself, I knew instantly that we were going to help. I'm blessed to be married to an animal lover who trusts my instincts, and Paul was perfectly fine with my decision to get Maggie home.

As always, the network had cross posted her picture, but as soon as the three-day stray hold was up, I was waiting at the shelter to take her home. I'd actually gone the day before, I was so excited and concerned for her, but it was a Sunday so they weren't doing placement. We promised to be a long-term "hospice" foster due to her age. In rescue parlance that means she will not have to be moved around anymore. She could settle in with us and it would be permanent.

We really don't know why she ended up in the shelter. The local animal control had a report of a stray running the streets, and picked her up. She had no collar, and no microchip.

This dog was sweet and sassy even at 10 *(or 12 or 14, we can't really know)* with only half her teeth. She was skinny, so we think she'd been out for a little while. We speculated that she'd slipped out when her owner left, or maybe her owner got sick and an ambulance came, or maybe she just dug a hole under her fence. It really doesn't matter; I'll ask her in Heaven what happened.

Maggie knew she was home as soon as I slipped on the halter. The picture of her settling into the little dog bed in the passenger seat of my car shows her smiling! She gave a big sigh and curled up.

At home, she said hello to Caleb, who couldn't have cared less *(until she stole his spot on my lap occasionally)*. She and Sarah became immediate besties, and once Sarah likes a visiting dog, or human, Toby is usually okay too.

Maggie spent about two weeks learning the ropes. She never knew she was only 11 pounds. She took over as the alpha, as most dachshunds will do. She figured out how to tell me when she wanted out, knew that the door opening to the utility room usually meant mom was coming out with a chicken treat, and that if she bounced high enough, I'd see her and put her on the couch.

Maggie and Sarah played like they were similarly sized. Tiny Maggie, climbing all over 75-pound Sarah up on mom & dad's bed. We always supervised carefully, but Sarah was really gentle. Maggie would get so aggressive and bouncy, though, that we had to make sure she didn't fall off! And Maggie chased Sarah around the yard!

And just a few adorable times she did chase Toby around the house. I am so glad to have that one video, where there were both slapping the floor with their front feet, and enjoying each other on a hot day when we couldn't do much outside. Mind you, Toby is a gentle giant at 100 pounds, so it's a pretty funny sight.

Even Pearl the cat didn't mind having her there, but I don't think they got close!

We got Maggie in October, and by February the pandemic hit us and in a way that timing was great. February to August *(when she went Home to the Rainbow Bridge)* I got to spend a lot of time with her while working from home. Despite the awfulness of the situation with COVID-19, I treasure that time with my funny girl.

One of her favorite things was to roll around in the grass; she'd either be dragging her belly along the grass, or roll over and chew on her own legs. In this era of smart phone cameras, you can imagine how many hundreds of photos and videos I have!

But Maggie was really sick. I switched from foster to adopter almost immediately because I wanted to use my own veterinarian for her. There were two surgeries for her teeth in a span of about three months, and her spine was shot. She needed quite a bit of pain medicine, which was somewhat of a daily ordeal because she was too smart to just take the pill pocket. She couldn't even use the doggie stairs to get on the bed or couch.

Maggie was careful to jump off the bed when she had to potty in the middle of the night, which was frequent. We put lots of doggie pads out for her.

One memory that will never leave me is the night she taught me that dachshunds like to be under the covers with you. It's hard to describe how she communicated to me...looking me in the eye, and then lifting the edge of the covers a little with her nose, and looking at me again. She was asking permission; "Mom, may I please come under with you?" It was precious, and became our routine.

Then, the light started to dim a little in her bright blue eyes, and her pain increased. One day, she was just keening from the pain, and she just wouldn't make it through another surgery, so we had to let her go. I sobbed for months, because I didn't get enough time with this precious girl.

MAGGIE TAUGHT ME A LOT ABOUT LOVING YOUR LIFE JUST AS IT IS. She had a truly joyful spirit, and she didn't wait to be accepted. She just jumped right in to become a part of the family. The lesson, I think, is to ASSUME THE BEST of everyone in your life. Your family, your boss, your employees. She didn't waste time deciding to be one of us and have fun. No matter the differences in breed and size and age, she enjoyed the company of every member of our family. When I wasn't home, she cuddled right up to Paul, or curled up next to Sarah. We were all for one and one for all in her mind. We could all learn from that; not worrying about how someone is different from us and just make a relationship and be friends. There's a lot about diversity out there right now, but first, maybe we can just think about loving each other the way Maggie showed us.

She also didn't waste a minute. Of course, I don't know what animals really understand about their own longevity, but if she knew she was sick it didn't stop her. She jumped right into her own joy and loved every minute of her time with us. She used up all of her energy every day just having a good time. I guess you could say we behaved that way too, loving her as if she'd always been with us and taking care of her the same way as if she'd be with us forever.

She didn't spend any time "evaluating" whether we were good enough for her, she just loved us and loved her life. There wasn't a moment lost to worry about what tomorrow would bring; she just got the most out of every single day. I think that is a great lesson for everyone! Just get the most out of today, and don't waste time worrying about tomorrow. Of course, as a planner, I'm not advocating you don't have a plan, but you don't have to worry every day. Make the plan and then stick to it so you can work each day to its fullest. Maggie never held back, never hesitated and never hesitated to play with her friends.

As far as I could tell, she didn't look back, or ever seem to be nostalgic to find her old family – she never tried to leave, as some strays do.

And, she had fun. She got up every day happy, even on her last day. She ran and played hard, and slept hard, and relished every bit of food and treats. That carefree nature seems like a good way to approach life, because we only get one shot at this. Why not have some fun?

Finally, Maggie spoke to us in the way some dogs do. Her gorgeous eyes were full of expression, and she used her body language *(like Angel did)* and funny little barks to tell us what she needed. Communication is the key to all successful relationships, in my opinion. Since every business is made up of many and varied relationships, we can learn from Maggie to try every method and be persistent to be sure our message is communicated in a way that everyone understands.

Maggie lived her life in love and we surrounded her with love until the last moment before she left for Heaven. I always try to hold my fur babies in that last moment, and even in that situation her eyes were on me with love. She knew her place with us and that even at the vet's office she was safe in my arms. I can't wait to see her again.

LISA H. HARRINGTON

# ABOUT THE AUTHOR

Lisa has over 35 years' experience in leadership, including many years in the C-suite as CEO, COO, CMO & EVP and more. Specific areas of experience include strategy planning, vision mapping, corporate alignment to strategy, culture change, executive coaching, management and operations. She has earned eight certifications: CPCU, CAM, CRIS, CAE, AAM, AAI, AIAM and AIP. Her B.A. degree in Management and Spanish was earned at the Miller College of Business at Ball State University.

She values Truth, Friendship, Service & Grace and is a regular contributor to several magazines, a leader on her church council, and an animal welfare advocate.

She resides in Southlake, Texas near Ft. Worth with her husband and many four-legged loved ones.

## *Additional Publications & Where to Follow Lisa*

**TAKING IN STRAYS:**
Leadership Lessons From Unexpected Places
*(Softback & Kindle available through Amazon.com)*

**TakingInStrays.com**

AbidingStrategy.com
linkedin.com/company/abiding-strategy
facebook.com/AbidingStrategy

## *About her business name: Sapphire Enterprises, LLC*

### *d/b/a Abiding Strategy*

Foundations are important to all of us, and the analogy of a strong foundation fits well with *my purpose to help businesses build a strong foundational strategy so they can make a real difference in the world.*

For me, *my FAITH is the* CORNERSTONE *of my existence.* The CORNERSTONE *(foundation stone or setting stone) is the first stone set in the construction of a masonry* FOUNDATION. All other stones will be set in reference to this stone, thus determining the position of the entire structure.

> Isaiah 28:16, "Therefore this says the Lord God: 'Behold, I lay in Zion a stone for a foundation, a tried stone, a precious cornerstone, a SURE FOUNDATION."

When I was building the business in 2009, trying to decide how to name the business, I decided that I would do research about FOUNDATIONS.

Great communication, planning & culture are keys to having a good foundation for a business. The human spirit must also be acknowledged for a business to succeed. I have built my practice on these foundational concepts.

According to the book of Revelation, jasper and SAPPHIRE are said to be the foundations of heaven. As a Christian, and hoping for heaven, this resonated for me.

Sapphire is my birthstone. But more importantly, it's mentioned in a message of hope:

> Isaiah 54:11 — "O thou afflicted, tossed with tempest, and not comforted, behold, I will lay thy stones with fair colors, and lay thy foundations with sapphires."

Sapphire is also mentioned as a part of the foundation of Heaven:

> Revelation 21:19 — "And the foundations of the wall of the city were garnished with all manner of precious stones. The first foundation was jasper; the second, sapphire; the third, a chalcedony; the fourth, an emerald; ..."

My birthstone, sapphire, is one of the precious stones used in *the foundation of heaven!*

I'm a big Star Trek fan because of the unification of planet earth and all humans, regardless of race, etc., — it's such a compelling story. So, the use of the word *enterprises* is also a little nod to who I am as a business owner and the things that influenced me as I grew up.

I was excited to hear that the word "enterprises" in combination with sapphire was available as a business name in the state of Texas when I set up my LLC.

The d/b/a Abiding Strategy also reflects my desire to help my clients create a strategy that will stand the test of time. I chose the word Abiding because of John 8:31-32, and because 'to abide' means 'to endure.' That's what I want for my clients; I can help them leave legacies. The images in the Abiding Strategy logo are meant to evoke feelings of legacy and striving for improvement. The wave is reminiscent of the philosophy of continuing improvement and a never ending wave of forward motion. The cross-like symbol reflects our desire for exploration as in points of the compass, and the reflection of a human stretched out seeking guidance.